Business Talk English

Stuart J. Dean

2. Auflage

Haufe.

Contents

Vorwort

Die Globalisierung und die neuesten Entwicklungen in der Kommunikationstechnolgie eröffnen Unternehmen aller Branchen und Größen bisher ungeahnte Möglichkeiten, international tätig zu werden. Wie jeder weiß, hat sich Englisch längst als Lingua franca des weltweiten Business etabliert. Sei es in Besprechungen, Diskussionen, Präsentationen, Verhandlungen, beim Small Talk oder einfach nur, um mit den Kunden in Kontakt zu bleiben – heutzutage ist es unverzichtbar, die korrekten englischen Ausdrücke und Wörter schnell zur Hand zu haben.

Dieser TaschenGuide enthält viele praktische Beispiele, Sätze und Erklärungen, die Ihnen in jeder Business-Situation weiterhelfen. Um einen zusätzlichen Trainingseffekt zu erzielen, ist das gesamte Buch auf Englisch geschrieben. Nützliche Worterklärungen auf Deutsch erleichtern das Verständnis. Weil die Sprache von kulturellen Faktoren beeinflusst wird, bekommen Sie auch nützliche interkulturelle Tipps und Erklärungen, welche Etikette-Regeln Sie sprachlich einhalten sollten. Dieses Buch ermöglicht es Ihnen, Ihr Business-Englisch schnell zu erweitern, verbessern oder aufzufrischen und ist daher ein wertvolles Nachschlagewerk für alle Gelegenheiten.

Ich wünsche Ihnen viel Erfolg bei Ihren internationalen Geschäften.

Stuart Dean

Let's Talk Business

Nearly all aspects of international business involve talking; to customers, suppliers, partners, colleagues or even the media.

This chapter will help you be prepared for the most common business situations e.g.:

- introducing yourself (page 8),
- telephoning (page 11),
- meetings (page 21), negotiations (page 31), presentations (page 35) and conferences (page 41),
- job interviews (page 46).

Tips for effective communication in English

You may already know many of the things that should be done in order to effectively prepare yourself for a business situation in a foreign language. Yet most people do not do them. Take a close look at the following list the next time before you go to a business meeting. Then make a conscious effort to try them out. You will be surprised how much they can help you to communicate effectively.

Some DOs

- Prepare vocabulary and phrases for important meetings and events. Check any difficult words in advance. Make notes to take with you.
- Ask people to speak slowly. English speakers may forget that you are a "non-native" speaker and sometimes need to be reminded of this several times!
- Having good eye contact with the person you are speaking to often helps communication. Non-verbal communication (body language) plays an important part in the communication process. It helps us to understand what is being said and also gives us important feedback as to whether we have been understood. At a meeting, try and choose a seat where you can easily see all other participants and have good eye contact.
- If you are listening to a presentation or attending a training course, try and sit at the front of the room near the

speaker. Don't hide at the back, where it will be more difficult to hear and understand what is being said.

Some DON'Ts

- Don't expect to follow every single word; otherwise you will soon get frustrated! Remember that when having a group conversation in your mother tongue you may also not always catch every single word that is said.
- Don't try to translate every word. There is no time for this. By the time you have translated everything, the group will be discussing a new topic!
- Don't be afraid to say you don't understand something. Useful expressions for this are given on page 26.
- Groups of English speakers may use slang expressions that you do not know. Again, don't be afraid to ask for an explanation!
- English speakers love abbreviations and acronyms. You may hear whole sentences made up of them! Don't be afraid to ask for an explanation. You will find a list of some common abbreviations and acronyms on page 115.
- You will often be speaking English with other non-native speakers from around the world. This can present additional challenges. Pronunciation will vary and it may take you time to adjust. Don't be afraid to tell the other person that you are having difficulty understanding them.

Introducing yourself

There are many business situations where you have to introduce yourself and talk about your company and job, for example at meetings, training courses, workshops, and conferences. Introductions can be very difficult, particularly in another language. The language used is fairly formal and the following section will help you be prepared for this. Many of these phrases are also useful in other situations, for example, when socialising.

Different ways of introducing yourself

Examples

Good morning everyone. My name is Susanne Faulhaber from CSF Systems in Berlin. We develop and market software for the travel industry. I joined the company in 2004. I'm responsible for the company's international sales, which means that I spend most of my time travelling throughout Europe. I manage a team of 6 people.

I'm Bernd Schönfelder, Product Manager at Amitek GmbH, where I have been working since 2001. Amitek produces parts for the automotive industry. We are based in Munich and we are one of the largest engineering companies in Bavaria. Before joining Amitek, I worked for a smaller engineering company in Ingolstadt. I'm married with two children aged 4 and 8.

I'm Jens Bauer and I work for Arabella Services in Hamburg. The company plans and manages corporate events for large multinational companies. I work in operations and I am responsible for ensuring that events run smoothly and within budget. I have worked at Arabella Services since leaving college in 2005. Hamburg is a great place to live because in my free time I can get into my boat and go sailing. And it gives me the opportunity to go swimming and listen to some great jazz in my free time.

Your name and company

- My name is ... / I'm ...
- I work for ... *(not "am working for")*
- I'm sales manager for ... (*you are the only sales manager*)
- I'm an account manager at ... (*you are one of several account managers*)
- The company produces software / machines / ...
- We develop (*or:* we market) ...
- I'm a freelance consultant / journalist.

Your work and responsibilities

- I'm responsible for European operations / I look after ...
- I work in banking. (*alternatives:* marketing, sales, accounting, product development, research, HR etc.)
- I manage a team of 8 people.
- I support our sales team.
- My job involves ...
- I report to the Business Development Director.

Job titles

It is often difficult to translate German job titles and you may have to use a different job title when talking in English. The most important thing is to choose a title that reflects your position and level of responsibility. You will find that the word "manager" is used more often in English than in German. In international business, a manager title is normal if you are the only person responsible for a particular key function or activity in your company; for example "Marketing Communications Manager" instead of "Marketing Communications Specialist".

How long you have been with your current company

- I have been working for Whitehouse Electronics since 2003 / for 4 years.
- I have worked at Whitehouse Electronics since 2003. (*not "am working at"*)
- I joined Whitehouse Electronics in 2003.

About you personally

- In my free time I enjoy reading, cooking and playing the piano.
- Outside of work I enjoy in-line skating and Nordic walking.
- I'm very keen on football and support our local team.
- I'm married with two children and live in Kiel.

The use of first names when talking to colleagues, business partners and even customers is standard practice (normal) throughout the English-speaking world. It does not imply any special relationship. Using only your family name / surname may create barriers in business relationships. When introducing yourself or meeting someone for the first time, it is recommended to use both your first and family name. Many English speakers will then automatically address you by your first name; others may continue to use your family name until invited to call you by your first name. To invite someone to call you by your first name, simply say, for example, "Please call me Gabi"; or to ask someone if it is OK to use their first name, "May I call you David?".

Useful vocabulary:

Please note that the German translations given in this TaschenGuide relate only to the specific situations described in the sections where they appear.

socialising:	unter Leuten sein / Kontakte knüpfen / Kontakte pflegen
market something:	etwas vermarkten oder verkaufen
automotive industry:	Automobilbranche
corporate events:	Firmenveranstaltungen

Telephoning

Despite the growth in email, many customers still prefer to talk to someone personally, rather than communicate in writing; it's often quicker to resolve a problem this way and helps to build good customer relationships. English speakers put particular importance on "politeness" when telephoning. This section provides you with the necessary phrases and vocabulary to make telephoning fun and effective.

Calling someone

When making a telephone call it's advisable to be well prepared! If your call involves discussing figures or dates, spend a few moments thinking about how to say them in English before you dial. Telephoning is sometimes difficult because we are not able to use non-verbal communication or body language to help us.

Example: The person you are calling is not there

A: Good morning, Euro Exhibitions, Peter Jones speaking, how can I help you?

B: Good morning, could I speak to Alison Holvey please?

A: Certainly. I'll put you through. Can I ask who's calling?

B: Yes, my name is Peter Schneider from Hamtek in Cologne.

A: Thank you, Mr Schneider; I'm putting you through now... I'm sorry her line's busy at the moment. Would you like to hold?

B: No, I'm sorry I have to make another call. Would it be possible for her to call me back as soon as possible, it's rather urgent?

A: No problem! If you give me your telephone number where she can reach you, I'll leave a note for her to call you.

B: Thank you. My direct line is "zero zero four nine" for Germany, "two two one, two four seven, eight nine double three" (0049 – 221 - 247 8933)

A: Thank you Mr Schneider. Can I just check how you spell your last name?

B: Sure, it's with a "c"; "s – c – h - n -e - i -d - e - r"

A: Thanks. I'll make sure she calls you as matter of urgency.

B: Thanks, goodbye.

You will often be asked to spell your name and sometimes be asked for other information such as your address. You can practice spelling your name and address using the English phonetic spelling shown on page 121. Be careful! Several letters of the alphabet are easily confused (e.g. German "i" and English "e" and the consonants "t" and "d").

Identifying yourself

- Good morning / afternoon my name is ... from ...
- This is Anton Müller from GBS in Munich.

Speaking to a particular person

- Could I speak to Gill Morris please?
- Could you put me through to ...
- Please could I speak to ...
- Is it possible to speak to your Managing Director please?

Purpose of the call

- I'm calling about ... (*or:* I'm calling with regard to ...)
- I would like to speak to someone about ...

Leaving a message

- Please could you ask her/him to call me? My number is ...
- Please could you let him/her know that I called?
- I would appreciate it if someone could call me back as soon as possible.

The person you are trying to call is not there or is busy

- When would be the best time to reach him/her?
- When would it be convenient for me to call back?

Finding out who you are speaking to

English speakers do not automatically give their names when calling to speak to someone, so be prepared to ask for this information.

Example

C: Good morning, could I speak to Peter Müller in your IT Department please?

D: Certainly, may I ask who's calling please?

C: Yes, my name is John Short from NJT Computer Systems in Birmingham

D: Thank you Mr Short, I'm putting you through now.

To find out who is calling

- Sorry, could/may I ask who I'm speaking to please?
- I'm sorry; I didn't catch your name.
- Please could you give me your name?
- Who am I speaking to please?
- May I ask who's calling

Telephone numbers are usually presented as individual numbers by English speakers. The numbers are also grouped differently. For example 23 25 267 as 232 5267, spoken "two three two, five two six seven"
More information about numbers can be found in the Appendix on page 118.

Example: You do not know who you need to speak to

A: Hello, is that Palmer & Whitehouse Electronics?

B: Yes it is: How can I help you?

A: I'm calling from Hamtek in Cologne and would like to talk to someone about one of your products.

B: Is it a price enquiry or a technical problem?

A: I just need some general information.

B: I see. I'll put you through to someone in our sales department who will be able to help you. May I ask who's calling?

A: Yes. My name is Peter Schneider.

B: Thank you Mr Schneider, I'm putting you through now.

Getting to speak to the right person

- I would like to talk to someone about ...
- I have a technical question concerning ...
- I need some general information about ...
- I'd like to speak to someone who can give more information about ...
- I'm not sure who I need to speak to, but I need some information about ...

Receiving a call

You may answer the telephone and be surprised by someone unexpectedly speaking English. Some English speakers will automatically assume that you understand and speak fluent English!

Beispiel

A: Transtechnik Leipzig, Langner, guten Tag – wie kann ich Ihnen helfen?

B: Good afternoon; is that the Transtechnik?

A: Yes it is. How can I help you?

B: We are a company based in New Zealand producing electronic products for the agricultural industry. I found your company in the Internet and noticed that you also manufacture and distribute electronic devices. We're looking for a European partner and I would like to speak to someone about this.

A: You really need to speak to our Business Development Manager, Bernhard Kühn. Unfortunately he's not in the office today. Can I take your name and telephone number and get him to call you?

B: Yes, that would be great. My name is Robert Davis and my direct number is + ("plus") 64 6 434 5851. That's six four for New Zealand, followed by the area code and telephone number. However, it may be difficult for him to reach me because of the 12-hour time difference.

A: In that case, could I suggest that you send him a short email with your contact details? I'm sure he will then reply to you as soon as he can.

B: OK that sounds fine. Can you give me his email address please?

A: Yes sure. It's Bernhard "dot" Kühn (spelt K U E H N) at Transtechnik "dot" d e.

B: Sorry, is that Bernhard with an H?

A: Yes it is.

B: Fine, I'll send him an email today. Perhaps you could also let him know that I'll be contacting him.

A: Yes of course. Thank you for calling Mr Davis.

B: Thank you. Goodbye.

Answering the telephone and identifying yourself

How you answer the telephone will depend on your company's own policy for answering the telephone, but it is usual for English speakers to identify themselves by their first and family or last name when taking/receiving external calls and to offer a short greeting. Giving only your last name is usually considered impolite. Some English speakers may even just give their first name when they call you: For example,

"Hello, this is Joanne speaking from Travel Nationwide in Boston".

Answering a call

- Hamtek Autoteile, Peter Schneider speaking; how can I help you?
- Good afternoon, Peter Schneider speaking.

Asking for clarification

- Could you tell me what it's about please?
- May I ask what it's concerning?
- Could you give me a little more information?

Checking information

- I'm sorry; I didn't catch that. Please could you repeat it?
- Please could you repeat that?
- I'm sorry; the line is very bad and I can't hear you very well.
- I'm sorry; I didn't catch your name. (Could you repeat it for me please?)
- Please could you spell that for me?
- May I just check that I've understood you correctly? Is it a technical or sales enquiry?

Arranging to call back

- Is it OK if I call you back in a few minutes/this afternoon /tomorrow?
- Please can I give you a call back later?
- Can I get back to you on that?
- When would be the best time for me to call you back?
- When is the best time to call her/him?

Keeping people waiting

Sometimes a caller may have to wait to speak to you (you are talking on the other line) or you may need to keep someone waiting while you search for information (find a file or document, ask a colleague something etc.). Politeness is very important to English speakers. Here are some useful phrases:

- Sorry to keep you waiting.
- Thank you for holding.
- I'm sorry to have kept you waiting. How can I help you?
- Would you mind holding the line while I get the file out?
- Rather than keep you waiting, would it be OK if I call you back in a few minutes?
- Peter Schneider's line is busy at the moment. Would you like to hold?

Telephone conferences

Regular telephone conferences are common in many international companies. Taking part in a telephone conference can be very hard work and frustrating. Please remember that native English speakers also have trouble understanding each other in conference calls.

Example

M: As facilitator for today's telephone conference let me begin by introducing myself ... So we all know who's on the line, can I ask everyone to briefly introduce themselves. Let's start with Paris.

P: Hi everyone, I'm Jean Paul from the office in Paris. Many of you know me from previous telephone conferences.

M: Thanks Jean Paul. Do we have anyone in Budapest today?

B: Yes, this is Réka Takács from Hungary. This is my first international telephone conference, so please be patient if I have problems understanding you!

M: Please don't be afraid to ask me or anyone else to repeat themselves during the meeting. That applies to all of you! Is anyone dialling in from the US or is it too early?

N: Yes, New York is already wide awake! I came into the office two hours early this morning. I'm Gwen Rogers by the way for those of you who don't know me. Is anyone else out there?

M: ... OK let's get started shall we. Item 1 on your agendas is our usual project update ...

Some phrases that you might need

– I would like to begin by asking everyone to introduce themselves.

- Please do not use the loudspeaker on your phone. The background noise makes it difficult to hear what is being said.
- Sorry, I'm having trouble hearing you – please could you repeat that?
- The line is very bad – I'm going to hang-up and dial in again.
- Sorry, could I ask the last speaker to identify himself again. I'm not sure who was speaking!
- Has someone got their loudspeaker on, I'm getting feed-back.

Useful vocabulary:

involve something:	mit etwas verbunden sein
figures:	Zahlen
put someone through:	jemanden durchstellen / verbinden
the line's busy:	die Leitung ist besetzt
rather urgent:	ziemlich dringend / eilt etwas
leave a note:	einen Zettel hinterlegen / eine Notiz hinterlassen
direct line:	Durchwahl
land line:	Festnetz
mobile (phone) / cell phone:	Mobiltelefon / Handy
When would it be convenient?	Wann würde es (Ihnen) passen?
not catch something:	etwas nicht mitbekommen
price enquiry:	Preisanfrage
assume:	davon ausgehen
manufacture:	herstellen / produzieren / anfertigen
a call back:	Rückruf
get back to someone:	auf jemanden zurückkommen

keep someone waiting:	jemanden warten lassen
get the file out:	die Unterlagen / die Akten / den Vorgang heraussuchen
that applies to all of you:	das gilt für alle
two hours early:	zwei Stunden früher (als üblich)

Meetings

"I spend all my time in meetings these days and don't have any time left to do my own job anymore!"

Most of us spend a lot of time in various kinds of meetings, including customer meetings, departmental meetings, project meetings, internal meetings and company meetings. This section covers expressions that you need for effective business meetings in English.

Client / customer meetings: breaking the ice

It's normal to exchange a few "pleasantries" (polite or humorous remarks designed to make the other person feel welcome) before getting down to the main business of the day. Here are some typical expressions:

- Thanks for coming today; how was your journey?
- Did you manage to find us OK?
- How was your flight?
- May I offer you a coffee before we start?

- Can I get you anything before we start – coffee, water ...?
- How's the weather in Sweden at the moment?

It is also normal to make general small talk before a meeting begins. Examples and expressions for making small talk are given on pages 81-87.

At the start of a meeting

Example

Chairperson: Before we start, I would like to ask someone to take the minutes of today's meeting... Do I have any volunteers? Oh, Thank you Brian. Does everyone have a copy of the agenda that was circulated last week? Good. We have a lot to get through today, so if anyone has any other issues they would like to raise, please do this at the end of the meeting when we come to "any other business". Also, please refrain from using mobile phones. If you need to make any personal calls, please try and do this during the breaks. Thank you.

OK, let's start with item one...

Some expressions that you might need

Function	Expression
1 Greetings	▪ A very warm welcome to you all. ▪ Firstly, I'd like to thank everyone for coming. ▪ I'll try and keep the meeting as brief as possible so that we can finish on time.
2 Making general comments	▪ Just a few formalities before we begin … ▪ A couple of general points: … ▪ Please turn off your mobile phones, toilets are at the end of the corridor … ▪ Does anyone have a problem if we speak English?
3 Introductions	▪ Before we start, let me begin by introducing myself … ▪ So that we all know who everyone is, can we quickly go round the table and introduce ourselves …
4 Explaining what the meeting is about	▪ The purpose of today's meeting is to … ▪ This morning's meeting is about … ▪ We are here today to discuss …
	▪ The aim of this afternoon's meeting is to …

5 Getting down to business	▪ Does anyone have any questions before we start? ▪ Does everyone have a copy of the agenda? ▪ OK, let's get down to business. ▪ Let's begin with the first item on the agenda, which is ... ▪ Turning to the first item on today's agenda, we need to discuss ... ▪ To start with, I'd like to discuss ...

During a meeting

Example: Keeping the discussion focussed

I think we're getting off the point here. I know that this matter is important to you all, but it's not what we are here to talk about today. Let's talk about this at the end and, if need be, set up a separate meeting for this. Let's move on to item 4, after which will make a short break for coffee.

Some expressions that you might need

Function	Expression
1 Keeping to the agenda	▪ I think we should move on to the next point. ▪ I think we're getting sidetracked here. Can we please stick to the point?

	▪ I'm not sure that's relevant to the issue in question. Perhaps we can discuss this outside of the meeting?
2 Discuss something later on	▪ That's a very good point, but can we talk about it at the end of the meeting? ▪ I think that's really a separate issue. Can we leave that until the end? ▪ I think you've made a very good point: can we come back to it later? ▪ Can we deal with that off line?
3 Before a break	▪ Just before we break for lunch, I'd just briefly like to talk about ... ▪ Before we have coffee, can I just say ... ▪ To finish off this morning's session, let's discuss item ....
4 A new point	▪ I think we also need to talk about ... ▪ We also need to consider ...
5 Having your say	▪ If I may just say something: ▪ Could I just add that ... ▪ I would just like to point out that ...
6 Getting agreement / reaching a decision	▪ Let's try and reach agreement on this. Can I have a show of hands from those of you who are in agreement with the proposal?

	▪ Are we all agreed that this is the right way forward? ▪ Do I have everyone's agreement on this? ▪ Do we have consensus on this?
7 Bringing the meeting to a close	▪ Just before we finish, does anyone have anything else they wish to raise? ▪ I think we've covered everything and would suggest we now finish the meeting. ▪ I think that's all we need to discuss this afternoon. Let's call it a day!

Example: At the end of a meeting

C: Before we finish, does anyone have any other business they would like to talk about? ...

B: Yes, I'd like to remind everyone about our company open day on Saturday June the 13th. We still need volunteers to act as guides and help on the information desk. Please can you remind staff in your department about this?

C: Thank you Barbara. If no one has anything else then I suggest we call it a day. Thanks everyone and have a good evening!

If you don't understand or follow something

– I'm sorry, but would you mind repeating that again please?

- I didn't catch the last point you made: Please could you explain that again?
- Would you mind explaining that again a little more slowly please?
- Could you explain that in more simple terms please?
- Is it possible for you to explain it again for the benefit of the non-native English speakers present?

The English word 'protocol' is not used to describe the general record of what was said and agreed in a meeting: these are called "the minutes". Written agendas for and minutes of meetings are covered in the chapter on written communication.

How to express your opinion during a meeting

English speakers value politeness when expressing opinions, especially when this concerns other people's work or suggestions. Criticism is often made by firstly making a positive statement (what you think is good about the idea or proposal), followed by a specific criticism or alternative suggestion. There are cultural differences between British and North American speakers. Both place importance on politeness, but British speakers are generally much more reserved, especially when expressing dissent. North Americans are more straightforward and sometimes even appear impolite to the British! They do, however, place importance on positive feedback and criticism combined with an alternative solution.

Expressing agreement with / support for something or someone

The arrows in the following tables indicate the level of agreement or disagreement, e.g. ↑↑ = strongly agree, → = neutral, ↓↓ = strongly disagree.

↑↑	I totally agree with ...
↑↑	I'm in total agreement with this proposal / idea.
↑	I think it's a really good idea.
↗	I agree with Angela on this one.
↗	I also think this is a good idea.
→	I don't see any problems.

Expressing disagreement with / opposition to something or someone

In many English-speaking countries it is normal to offer an alternative solution or idea when expressing opposition to, or criticism of, something. Offering only criticism is regarded as negative. Here are some phrases to help you do this:

←	I don't really mind either way on this one.
↙	I think this proposal is OK, but I would like to see ... I'm not entirely happy with this. I like the idea, but perhaps we should look at ...
↙	Although I think this is a good idea, I'm not convinced that this is the best way forward. It may be better to ...

↓ I don't think this is a good idea at all. My suggestion would be ...

↓↓ I'm not really in agreement with any of this. Why don't we look at ...

↓↓ I'm not in favour of this proposal at all.

Having your say

Using a foreign language can make participation in a discussion more difficult. Here are some useful phrases for expressing your own ideas:

- I would just like to add that ...
- We need to talk about ...
- I think it's more important to consider ...
- I think we are getting sidetracked here. Returning to the issue in question ...
- In my opinion ...
- I would like to point out that ...

You may need to interrupt someone in order to have your say:

- I'm sorry but I have to stop you there ...
- Sorry to interrupt you, but ...
- May I just stop you there for a moment?
- May I just add something before you continue?

Useful vocabulary:

schedule a meeting:	eine Besprechung ansetzen
attend a meeting:	an einer Besprechung teilnehmen
reschedule a meeting:	eine Besprechung verlegen
postpone a meeting:	eine Besprechung verschieben
agenda:	Tagesordnung
circulate the agenda:	Tagesordnung verteilen
minutes:	Protokoll
take the minutes:	Protokoll führen
approve the minutes:	Protokoll annehmen
minute taker:	Protokollant, Protokollführer
chairman/chairperson:	Leiter(in) einer Besprechung
attendee:	Teilnehmer
participant:	Teilnehmer
pleasantries	höfliche Floskeln
Did you manage to find us OK?	Haben Sie uns gut gefunden?
issue:	Angelegenheit, Thema
refrain from something:	etwas unterlassen
go round the table:	in der Reihenfolge der Sitzplätze jeden etwas fragen
purpose:	Zweck, Ziel
get down to business:	zur Sache kommen / zum Geschäftlichen kommen
get off the point:	vom Thema weg kommen
move on to the next item:	zum nächsten Punkt weitergehen
get sidetracked:	abgelenkt werden
deal with something off line:	etwas außerhalb des Meetings besprechen
raise something:	etwas vorbringen
Let's call it a day:	Lasst uns Schluss / Feierabend machen
I don't mind either way:	Es ist mir egal (*nicht abwertend, im Sinne von: Ich bin neutral; beides ist mir Recht*).

Negotiations

Almost everything we do involves negotiation. As well as negotiating formal contracts, we also negotiate individually with colleagues, business partners, customers, suppliers and even with our family and friends. Negotiation requires special language skills to make sure we achieve a satisfactory result. English is generally less direct than German. One important exception to this is in respect of money. North Americans in particular will openly talk about how much money they earn or how much a contract will cost.

What is negotiable?

Examples

	Typical questions and answers
Price	Buyer: Is there a discount for large orders? Seller: We could offer a 10% reduction in the unit price for orders of more than 2,000 units.
Quantity	S: Before we talk about the price, can you give me an idea of the quantity you require? B: Between 250 and 500. If we buy sufficient quantities for all our offices, we would expect a better price.
Delivery date	B: How soon would you be able to supply the goods? S: That depends on how quickly you place a definite order. We normally deliver within 4 weeks assuming that all components are in stock.
Payment	B: What are your terms of payment? S: We ask for a 25% advance payment at the time of

	confirming the order. The balance is payable within 30 days of the final invoice. B: What sort of discount could you offer if we were to settle the full amount in advance? S: I would need to check this with our Finance Director, but I'm sure we could come to some agreement.
Shipping costs / delivery costs	B: Does the price include delivery? S: No it doesn't. If you want us to cover transportation costs, I can arrange for a separate quotation to be sent to you.
Quality	S: The offer is based on our superior model, which most of our customers prefer. B: I'm not sure we need all of these features. What would a standard model cost?
Guarantee	B: What is the guarantee period? S: All our products are guaranteed for 12 months, including parts and labour. If anything goes wrong during this time, we will put it right free of charge. Should you require a longer warranty period, this is negotiable. Some clients opt for our 5-year guarantee which is subject to an additional premium at the time of purchase.
Service	B: What sort of service do you offer in the event of something going wrong? S: We provide technical support throughout Europe and have a network of local partners in each country. Our service hotline is also available 24 hours a day. B: Do you provide training? S: Yes, one of our trainers will visit your company to train your staff in how to use the system. We also have a hotline to deal with problems and questions by telephone.

Indicating you would like to negotiate

- Can we talk about the price / delivery date(s) / volume / quantity?
- Do you have any flexibility with regard to price?
- Is this offer negotiable?
- I think there are one or two issues that we need to discuss.
- How much room for negotiation is there?

Indicating you are willing to negotiate

- I'm sure we can come to an agreement on this.
- We might be able to meet you halfway.
- We do have some room to manoeuvre.

Negotiating

- We could (probably) reduce the price if you were to take a minimum number of 50 units.
- We can offer you a discount for large orders over 100 units.
- If we ordered a larger quantity, would you be able to reduce the unit price?

Closure

Negotiations can be long and detailed, but, unless you wish to work into the night, at some point you will need to bring the discussion to a close.

- Is that your very best offer?
- The best we can do is ...
- This is our final offer – we really can't go any lower on price.
- Do we have a deal?

Buying Time (Delaying)

- I think we need time to think about this.
- Can we come back to you on this?
- I will need to discuss this with my colleague(s) first.

Accepting

- I think we can live with this offer.
- I'm sure we can do business on this basis.
- Now I think we're talking business!
- Shall we shake on this? (*meaning:* to shake hands)

Declining

- I'm sorry but we can't accept your offer.
- I don't think we can work on this basis.
- Sorry, but we cannot accept these conditions.
- I'm afraid the offer is still not acceptable.

Useful vocabulary:

achieve:	erreichen
in respect of:	bezüglich
when purchasing goods or services:	beim Einkaufen von Waren und Dienstleistungen
discount:	Rabatt, Preisnachlass
require:	benötigen
assuming:	angenommen
balance:	Restbetrag
invoice:	Rechnung
settle:	begleichen
payment terms:	Zahlungsbedingungen
aftersales:	Kundenbetreuung
quotation:	Angebot, Preisangebot
decline	ablehnen
delay	verschieben
agree:	sich einigen
quotation:	Angebot
guarantee period:	Garantiezeit
warranty:	Gewähr, Garantie
provide support:	Unterstützung anbieten
meet halfway:	auf halbem Weg entgegenkommen
room to manoeuvre:	Spielraum

Presentations

Whether you are giving or listening to a presentation; if it's not in your mother tongue, then there will most certainly be additional challenges because of the language. You are probably familiar with words and phrases in your own specialist business area, but expressions for linking ideas and topics are also very important in presentations. This section includes vocabulary and expressions you will need for this.

Preparation / Organisation

Here are some useful expressions if you are preparing or organising a presentation:

- What audiovisual equipment do you require?
- I'll just need a beamer and a microphone. I'll bring my own laptop / computer with me.
- My presentation is on a CD which I will bring with me. Do you have a suitable laptop? I'll also need a flipchart – are you able to arrange this?
- I'd like to have about 15 minutes before the presentation to familiarise myself with the room and audiovisual equipment.
- Please can you make 70 copies of the presentation as handouts?

The presentation

Examples

The start of the presentation

Good morning ladies and gentlemen. Let me begin by introducing myself: I'm Anton Müller from BTF in Leipzig. I'm going to talk about new developments in production technology at our plant in Germany. There will be plenty of time for your general questions at the end, but please do not hesitate to interrupt me at any time during the presentation should you need clarification on any specific point.

I'd like to begin by presenting an overview of our production facilities at our factory in Leipzig. .... This slide shows the five basic processes we have ...

During the presentation

Having given you an overview of our current production technologies, I'd now like to talk about new developments in technology. This slide is a summary of BTF's current development projects, showing planned implementation dates.

Moving on, I would now like to tell you a little bit about ...

At the end of the presentation

And finally, here is another summary of our current development projects. I hope you have found the presentation interesting and I would be pleased to answer any questions that you might have. Thank you very much for your attention!

If you are the presenter

Purpose	Expression
Introducing a topic	▪ I'd like to start by talking about ... ▪ I'd like to begin by presenting an overview of ...
Finishing a topic	▪ Just one final point on this: ... ▪ Before we move on, I'd just like to say ...
Moving to the next topic	▪ Moving on to sales / technical issues / staffing implications etc.

	▪ Turning to the next point ... ▪ Let's now take a look at ...
Giving more detailed information	▪ Looking at this in more detail ... ▪ Let's take a closer look at this. ▪ I'll talk about this in more detail in a moment.
Background information	▪ Just to give you some background information about ... ▪ A little bit about the history of the project ... ▪ Some general information about ...
Difficult / complicated information	▪ Although this diagram looks very complicated, the main point to note is ... ▪ Don't be put off by this slide. The important thing here is ...
Dealing with difficult questions	▪ That's a very good question. May I come back to that at the end? ▪ That's a good point. Can I come back to you on that? ▪ Would you mind if we deal with all questions at the end? ▪ I don't have the answer to that now, but I'll certainly look into it and come back to you.

Finishing the presentation	▪ Lastly, I'd just like to talk about ... ▪ And finally, a summary of the main points: ... ▪ Finally, just to summarise the main points: ...

If you are listening to a presentation

Purpose	Expression
Problems hearing or seeing	▪ I'm sorry, but I can't hear you properly from here. Is it possible to do something about sound quality? ▪ I'm having trouble reading the slides / figures. Is it possible to make them any bigger / sharper?
Clarification	▪ I'm not sure I understood the last point. Please could you explain that again? ▪ I'm having trouble following your argument. Would you mind going through that once more? ▪ If I have understood you correctly, you're saying that ... ▪ I don't understand why ...
Challenging something	▪ Why do you say that ... ▪ Why is it that ...

	▪ How come there is/are ... ▪ Can you explain why ... ▪ Is there any reason for the ...
Telling the speaker what you would like to hear	▪ That's all very interesting, but what I'd really like to know is ... ▪ Please can you tell us something about ... ▪ One thing I don't think you've covered so far is ...
Positive feedback	▪ I found the presentation very interesting. Is it possible to get a copy of it? ▪ Thanks for the excellent presentation.

Useful vocabulary:

attend a presentation:	in einen Vortrag gehen
overview:	Überblick
summary:	Zusammenfassung
table:	Tabelle
chart:	Diagramm / Grafik
figures:	Zahlen
bullet point:	Aufzählungspunkt, Stichpunkt
target group:	Zielgruppe
aims:	Ziele
challenge:	Herausforderung
familiarise oneself with something:	sich mit etwas vertraut machen
plant:	Fabrik, Werk
slide:	Folie

take a closer look at something:	etwas genauer anschauen
in more detail:	näher eingehen
be put off by something:	sich abschrecken lassen
summarise:	zusammenfassen
so far:	bisher, bis jetzt

Trade fairs & conferences

These are important events for making new business contacts and cultivating existing ones. Two key skills required are being able to start and develop conversations, and describing your business activities or requirements effectively in a very short period of time. This section provides you with some useful expressions for making conversation with people. It will also help you prepare a short description of your company's products and services.

Example: At an exhibition stand (booth)

A: Hello! Are you familiar with our company's products and services? Can I help you with any more information?

B: I'm just having a general look around thanks.

A: I see. Are you looking for anything in particular? Perhaps one of our products could be of possible interest to you?

B: I'm not sure - what is it you actually do? I know the company name but am not sure what you sell.

A: We provide all kinds of packaging. Our main business is supplying packing material to companies running mail order services or Internet shops. Whether it's wine, fresh flowers, books, CDs or sports equipment; we specialise in offering a safe and cost-effective solution. And, if we don't have it in stock, we we'll source it or even produce it for you!

B: We have to send spare parts to clients and partners around the world. Avoiding breakages and damage in transit is always a big problem for us.

A: We know the problem very well. Many of our customers send high-value products worldwide. If you leave me your card, I can arrange for someone from our company to contact you, to talk about various alternatives. Obviously, there's no obligation, but you never know, we might even be able to offer something better and cheaper than what you are currently using!

Beginning a conversation

- Can I help you at all? Would you like some more information about our products and services?
- Would you like to know more about our company and what we do?
- How can I help you today? Are you looking for anything in particular?

Talking about your company

- We have offices in ...
- The company employs 5,000 people worldwide.
- Our European headquarters is in ...
- The group's head office is in ...
- We have four manufacturing plants in Germany.
- The company was established in 1985.
- We are a small family run business.
- We have subsidiary companies in ...
- We are part of the UPC Group.
- Our product range includes ...

A short introduction to your company and its products and services is often known as an elevator pitch or speech. More information about this is can be found in the chapter "Making a good first impression" on page 56.

Example: During the coffee break

A: How are you enjoying the conference? What did you think of the last speaker?
B: Oh, I think the conference is excellent. I really enjoyed the first session this morning, although I had problems following the last speaker. She spoke very quickly and softly.
A: Yes, I agree. I could hardly hear her sometimes. Are you here for all three days or just paying a flying visit?
B: I arrived last night, but unfortunately can't stay for the final podium discussion tomorrow afternoon. I have to leave at lunchtime for an appointment in Brussels. And you?
A: I'm here for all three days. Our company, CHZ Holdings, is one of the main sponsors. We are running a couple of workshops and also have an exhibition stand.
B: How has it been so far?
A: Yesterday was fairly quiet, but today it's a lot busier on the stand. What does your company do, if you don't mind me asking?
B: We specialise in outsourcing all kinds of business processes, from payroll to training and development, basically allowing companies to concentrate on their core business and buy in expertise where appropriate. Perhaps we could be of interest to your organisation?
A: Actually, I'm not the best person to speak to about that. You really need to speak to our Corporate Planning Manager, Raymund Jones. He's not here today, but if you could give me your business card, I'll pass it on to him.
B: Will he be here tomorrow?
A: Yes he should be here all day.
B: In that case, I'll try and catch up with him in the morning. Can I get you another coffee?
A: Oh, thank you: Yes please, that's very kind of you.

Expressing opinions about an event

↑↑ I thought the last presentation was really excellent!

↑ I think the standard of the speakers is extremely high this year.

↗ The programme is very interesting.

→ The conference is OK, but I would prefer to see more ...

↘ I'm disappointed that there ...

... is no time for questions.

... are so few practical examples.

... is too much emphasis on ...

↓ I'm not at all impressed by the speakers.

↓↓ I think the conference is very disappointing indeed.

Example: In the cafeteria

A: Excuse me, is this seat free?

B: Yes sure; sorry, let me just move my bag out of the way.

A: Thank you. It's great to sit down after walking around for such a long time! The exhibition gets bigger every year. Are you here as a visitor as well?

B: Yes, I'm a freelance journalist and am writing an article about the event for a trade journal. And you?

A: I work for a large supermarket chain. We're always looking for potential new suppliers and it's a good opportunity to catch up with all the latest developments in the retail industry. What trends will you be writing about then?

B: Oh, I've still only done a quarter of the exhibition. It's too early to say. No doubt the most important developments will be in technology. What do you think of the exhibition?

A: It's almost become too large. I got completely lost in Hall B and couldn't find the companies I was looking for. I prefer smaller, more specialist events. But I suppose most people find it convenient to have everything under one roof.

B: Yes, I agree: it is bigger than ever this year.

What is the purpose of your visit?

- I'm looking for new suppliers.
- I'm interested in the latest developments and new trends in the industry.
- We hope to find new business.
- I'm hoping to make some new business contacts.

What sort of events do you prefer?

- I prefer smaller and more specialist trade fairs.
- I would rather attend one big exhibition a year than spend time travelling to lots of other events.
- It's important to have lots of international companies.
- I like events that have certain days for trade visitors only: I don't like public days at all.
- For me, it's important to see the big names and market leaders.
- I don't like really big events because it's often difficult to find one's way around the exhibition.

Useful vocabulary:

delegate(s):	Teilnehmer
booth:	Messestand
exhibitor:	Aussteller
cultivate business contacts:	Geschäftskontakte pflegen
packaging:	Verpackung
supply:	liefern /beliefern??
mail order:	Versandhandel
avoid:	vermeiden
headquarters:	Zentrale
head office:	Hauptsitz
subsidiary company:	Tochtergesellschaft
product range:	Produktpalette
core business:	Kerngeschäft
buy in expertise:	Kompetenz / Fachwissen einkaufen
actually:	eigentlich
catch up with someone later:	mit jemandem zu einem späteren Zeitpunkt sprechen

Job interviews

Many international companies and organisations conduct job interviews in English. The following phrases will help you when interviewing someone in English and also when being interviewed as a candidate.

The object of any interview is to find out as much as possible about the other person / organisation. For this, you will need to ask "open" questions (those requiring a detailed answer) rather than "closed" ones (questions requiring you to answer just 'yes' or 'no'). Typical "open" questions begin with words like 'why', 'what' and 'how'. Avoid starting sentences with 'do', 'did' or 'are you ...' unless you are looking for a one word answer!

Standard interview questions

Here is a selection of the most common interview questions.

What made you apply for this job? / Why did you apply for this job?

- I'm looking for a new challenge.
- The job description is very interesting and I believe I have all the necessary skills and experience that you are looking for.
- I would like to work for a well-known international company like ...
- I'm looking for a job with more responsibility.
- I'd like to work in an English-speaking country.

Why do you want to change your job / employer?

- I'm looking for a new challenge.
- I'm ready to take on more responsibility.
- I'm looking for a more senior position.
- I would like to work for an international company.
- For personal reasons I would like to move to Boston.

What can you do for us?

– I believe that my skills and experience would be of value to your company, particularly my knowledge of ...
– I am sure that I can make a significant contribution to the (continuing) success of your company.
– As well as meeting the requirements given in your job advertisement, I also have experience in ...

What are your strengths and weaknesses?

– I'm a very well-organised person and good at time management. Because of my enthusiasm and motivation, I can sometimes be a little impatient.
– I'm a good team player but also capable of working on my own. I'm sometimes a perfectionist and therefore try to avoid spending too much time on any one task.
– I'm good with people and have the ability to motivate others. I set myself high standards and expect the same from colleagues.
– I'm a very logical person and do not usually panic. I'm good at remaining calm under pressure.

What do you like most about your current job / company?

– I enjoy the contact with customers.
– I particularly enjoy the contact with international suppliers.
– I like working in a team.

- I like the open and un-bureaucratic atmosphere.
- Everyone's personal input and contribution is valued.
- It's very varied and every day is different.

What don't you like about your current job / company?

- I think we suffer from the same problems faced by all large organisations. Communication can always be improved!
- It's rather chaotic sometimes, but this can also be stimulating.
- I really enjoy my job. There are some less interesting routine tasks, but I'm sure that's true of any job.

What would you describe as / what is your greatest achievement so far?

This is usually a professional success story (for example a project you have implemented, results you have achieved, changes you have implemented etc.) but may also be a personal achievement.

- I successfully implemented a new system for ...
- I successfully managed a project for ...
- I achieved a 10% increase in sales of ...
- I was the top salesman for Germany in 2006.
- I worked as part of a team on the implementation of a new system for ...
- Last year I cycled through the Alps all the way to Italy.

Tell us about yourself

This open question is usually an invitation to give a summary of your career, i.e. the companies where you have worked and what you have achieved.

- After leaving school, I worked for Whitehouse Electronics where I gained experienced working as a ...
- After leaving Whitehouse Electronics, I went to work at NJT Computer Systems.
- I began as a sales assistant before being promoted to supervisor.
- I was then promoted to Assistant Manager.
- I left Whitehouse Electronics to join NJT Computer Systems because I was looking for more responsibility.

What do you do outside work?

Employers are interested in what sort of person you are. Hobbies and other leisure activities are important and provide information about this.

- I'm very interested in music and play the saxophone in a band.
- I play a lot of sport and am a member of a local football team.
- I very much enjoy being a parent and spend a lot of time with my daughter / son / children.
- I enjoy travelling and learning about other cultures. India is one of my favourite countries.
- Last year I took up in-line skating and now do it several times a week.

When are you available? What is your period of notice?

How soon you can start a new job is very important to prospective employers and is a standard interview question.

- I have to give one month's notice to the end of the calendar month.
- I have to give four weeks' notice (*i.e. from the date you resign*).
- I have a three-month period of notice to the end of the quarter.

> Note: The German system of giving notice to the end of the quarter is not very common in English-speaking countries. You will need to explain this. Periods of notice are generally shorter than in Germany, particularly in the USA.

What sort of salary are you looking for? / What are your salary expectations?

Salaries in the UK, USA and other English-speaking countries are usually quoted and negotiated per annum (year) rather than per month. The salary range is often quoted in job advertisements i.e. in the UK, £25 – 35K meaning 25,000 to 35,000 pounds per year. Salaries are normally paid in 12 monthly instalments. Additional payments at Christmas and in the summer are not common. Many companies pay a 'basic' or 'fixed' salary and a variable amount depending on individual or company performance. The abbreviation OTE –

on target earnings – indicates the total salary that can be achieved.

- My current salary is 40,000 euros and I would be looking to improve on this.
- I currently earn 3,400 euros a month.
- My annual salary is around forty-five thousand euros and I would hope to improve on this.
- I think that forty thousand dollars would be reasonable for this position, given the level of responsibility and experience you are looking for.

Who can we contact for references?

- I've provided a list of references in my CV (*US* 'résumé').
- Please contact me first before taking up references.
- I would ask you not to contact my current employer.
- I can provide you with professional and personal references.

> The German "Zeugnis" system of testimonials is not generally used in English-speaking countries. Employers will ask to see certificates in respect of specific educational and professional qualifications, but will normally "take up" references after an interview. Job offers are often made in writing "subject to references". This means they will contact the people you have given as "referees" for their opinion(s) about you. It is normal to provide the names of two professional referees (e.g. previous employers or educational establishment in the case of first-time employment) and one personal referee (e.g. someone who has known you for a long period of time and has a good standing in the community).

Questions to ask at an interview

It's wise to be prepared to ask your interviewer(s) a few questions. Asking questions indicates your interest in the job and company and creates a good impression. Here are some typical questions you could ask:

- Does the company have its own pension scheme?
- Are there any other employee benefits?
- Do you have an employee training and development programme?
- What are the normal office hours?
- How much travelling does the job involve?
- What is the probation period? (*normally 6 months*)
- How soon do you expect to make a decision?
- How many other candidates will you be interviewing for this position?
- How will you notify the successful candidate?

Useful vocabulary:

certificates:	Urkunden, Zertifikate
skills and experience:	Kompetenzen und Praxiserfahrung
salary expectations:	Gehaltsvorstellung
covering letter:	Anschreiben, Begleitbrief
applicant:	Bewerber
senior position:	führende Position
be of value to someone:	wertvoll / nützlich für jemanden sein
a significant contribution:	bedeutender Beitrag

requirements:	Anforderungen
international suppliers:	internationale Lieferanten
personal input:	persönlicher Einsatz
valued:	geschätzt
increase of sales:	Absatzsteigerung
give one month's notice to end of the calendar month:	zum Monatsende kündigen
give four weeks' notice:	kündigen mit einer Frist von 4 Wochen
CV – Curriculum vitae / résumé:	Lebenslauf
take up references:	Referenzen einholen
referee:	Referenz
pension scheme:	betriebliche Altersversorgung
employee benefits:	Sozialleistungen
to notify:	mitteilen

The Customer is King

Many business situations are critical and success depends on finding exactly the right words and tone. How to say "no" without causing offence, reassure a customer and resolve a problem with a product or service are all key elements in doing international business.

This chapter will help you to find just the right phrase, e.g. for

- making follow-up calls (page 60),
- dealing with an angry customer (page 67),
- saying "no" politely (page 69)and complaining successfully (page 71), or
- issuing ultimatums and giving deadlines (page 74).

Making a good first impression

"You never get a second chance to create a first impression." Making a good first impression is essential in winning new customers and business. The elevator pitch (or elevator speech) is an American term. It is so called because it can be delivered in the short time you are riding in an elevator ("lift" in British English), i.e. 30 seconds or so. The elevator pitch is normally a short description of what you or your company does, highlighting the customer benefits. It is also used by entrepreneurs (people starting new projects or business opportunities) when pitching an idea to venture capitalists (third parties providing finance).

There are many different types of elevator speeches depending on the circumstances, for example what you are selling and who you are speaking to.

Example

"Our new company is called Sheet Music Unlimited, an e-commerce website that sells second-hand sheet music. There are currently no companies serving this niche market. We will generate traffic to the website by linking to other specialist websites catering for musicians (companies selling musical instruments, music organisations etc.) as well as through word-of-mouth.

Second-hand book sales via the Internet have been very successful and we see very many similarities. Our research indicates that many professional and amateur musicians would buy second-hand music if they knew where to find it. Our advanced search function is the key to success. Sheet Music Unlimited offers customers the opportunity to search on a wide range of musical criteria in both English and all major European languages. Easy online payment facilities will ensure that orders are dispatched within 48 hours.

We believe that the Internet offers a unique opportunity for us to exploit this specialist and currently highly fragmented market."

Your personal elevator pitch

It is essential to prepare an "elevator pitch" in advance and to memorise it. This is particularly important when you are speaking in a foreign language. Being well-prepared will allow you to deliver your elevator pitch anywhere and at anytime; e.g. at trade fairs, conferences, meetings, on aircraft or even when riding in an elevator! If you are working for a company selling products and/or services, typical elements of your pitch should be:

The market you are in

- Hamtek Autoteile is a supplier to the automotive industry.
- We are in the engineering business.
- We are in the consultancy business.

The products and services you are selling

- We provide a complete range of accounting software for business of all sizes.
- Our company produces machinery for the agricultural industry.
- We offer a full range of consultancy services for the health industry.

Your USPs (unique selling proposition)

These are characteristics of your products and services that differentiate them from those of your competitors. They give potential customers a reason to choose you rather than products or services from one of your rivals.

- We are able to supply software and documentation in most major European languages.
- We are the only company specialising in the area of ...
- Our products are all manufactured in-house and subject to strict German and industry quality controls.

The customer benefits

What does your product or service do for the customer? Do not confuse "benefits", i.e. things that improve or promote, with "features", i.e. functions and characteristics.

Customer benefits for B2B companies (business to business):

- We help customers to maximise the return on their investment in ...
- Our energy saving products help our customers reduce their production costs and thereby gain competitive advantage.
- Our specialist services allow companies to concentrate on their core business.
- We help companies to improve their profitability by ...
- Our products allow companies to be more responsive to changes in the market.

Customer benefits for B2C companies ("business to consumer")

- Our easy-to-assemble products make furniture more affordable to a wider market.
- We provide the most environmentally friendly washing machines currently available.

Useful vocabulary:

elevator pitch / elevator speech:	„Aufzugspräsentation" = ein Überblick einer Firma, Dienstleistung oder ein Produkt, der in einer kurzen Zeit (ca. 30 Sekunden) durchgeführt werden kann.
entrepreneur:	Unternehmer
pitch an idea:	eine Idee verkaufen
niche market:	Nischenmarkt
catering for something:	auf etwas ausgerichtet sein
word-of-mouth:	Mundpropaganda
dispatched within 4 hours:	versendet innerhalb von 4 Stunden
exploit a market:	einen Markt erschließen
complete range of products:	komplette Produktpalette
subject to:	gemäß
benefits:	Nutzen, Vorteile
features:	Eigenschaften
competitive advantage:	Wettbewerbsvorteil
be responsive to something/someone:	auf etwas / jemanden reagieren
easy-to-assemble products:	leicht zu montierende Produkte
affordable:	bezahlbar
environmentally friendly:	umweltfreundlich

Showing customer orientation

Customer service is very important in most English-speaking countries, particularly in the USA. Customer service does not just mean offering a special department to deal with problems and complaints, but involves customer-orientated attitudes and behaviour. By choosing the right words and tone, it is possible to turn a bad situation into one which the customer remembers in a positive way. Here are some typical situations involving good customer service:

Example

A: But I'm a regular guest in your hotel: I have always had an executive room in the past. Surely you can do something for me?

B: Mr Johnson, please rest assured that you are one of our most valued customers. Unfortunately, on this occasion we simply don't have any executive rooms available. I'll make a note of it in the computer and should the situation change, we'll ensure that you have first priority. When you arrive on Tuesday, please ask for me personally and I will see what we can do for you then. I can't promise anything, but we'll certainly do our very best to make sure you have an enjoyable stay with us.

The customer is important

- As one of our most valued customers, let me say how sorry I am about ...
- Our aim is to make sure that all are customers are entirely satisfied with our products / services at all times.
- Please rest assured that we are doing everything possible to resolve the situation.

Example

A: I still can't access my email or use the Internet. It's been like this all day and quite honestly it's not acceptable.

B: I'm very sorry for the inconvenience caused. We are doing everything possible to put things right. We're still working on the problem and hope to have it fixed in about 30 minutes.

Saying what you are doing now (the action has started and is still happening)

Use the following expressions to assure and convince the customer that you are trying to put things right as soon as possible:

- We're sorting it out now.
- We're working on the problem and hope to have things working again in about an hour.
- They are fixing it at this very moment.
- They're looking into the problem and will contact you as soon as it has been sorted out.

- We're investigating what happened and will contact you in the very near future.
- We're already dealing with the problem.

Example

A: I've been trying to get through to your reservations department all day but it is either engaged or there is no answer.

B: I'm very sorry that you've been having problems. We try to ensure that we have sufficient staff to deal with the volume of incoming calls at any one time. There are occasionally times when you may have to wait a little longer than usual, but it should always be possible to get through. If you give me your name and telephone number, I'll make sure that someone gets back to you on this as soon as possible.

Saying what action you will take next (the action has not yet begun)

Use these expressions to tell the customer what will be done to solve the problem:

- I will make sure this matter is dealt with as soon as possible.
- I will contact someone in our Operations Department right away and ask them to call you.
- If you leave me your name and telephone number, I'll ask someone to look into this and get back to you.
- I'll get someone on to this right away.

Offering general assistance

It's normal for English speakers to offer general help and assistance to customers. You can show that you are customer orientated by using the following expressions:

- If you need anything just let me know.
- Should you have any problems, please feel free to contact me.
- If I can be of any further help, please don't hesitate to contact me.
- Just let me know if you need anything else.
- If you have any queries, just give me a call.
- My name is Angela Smith and should you need any further assistance please just give me a ring.

Useful vocabulary:

inconvenience:	Unannehmlichkeit(en)
put things right:	Abhilfe schaffen
sort a problem out:	ein Problem lösen
at this very moment:	zurzeit
in the very near future:	in nächster Zeit
look into the problem:	das Problem untersuchen
investigate what happened:	untersuchen, was passiert ist
deal with the problem	ein Problem bewältigen

Follow-up calls

You sent a written quotation to a company 3 weeks ago and have so far not heard anything from them. Rather than send an email, you think it is better to give them a quick call. A telephone call allows you to maintain personal contact with the customer. But how do you make sure you sound friendly and professional on the telephone, without making the customer feel under pressure? English speakers tend to avoid asking direct questions when making follow-up calls about offers or quotations, unless they are calling to ask something specific about the detail of the offer.

Example

A: "I'm calling with regard to a quotation that we sent to you a few weeks ago. I just wanted to check that you have received it and to ask whether everything is OK.

B: Yes, we did receive your offer thank you. We're currently reviewing all offers and hope to make a decision in the next few days.

A: I see. Well if you do need anything else in the meantime or have any questions, please let me know.

B: Thank you, I'm sure we'll be in touch if we do. We hope to contact everyone by the end of the month, so please bear with us until then. Thanks for your call.

Following up on a letter or email

- We sent you a written quotation on the 25th of September and I just wanted to check you have received it and if everything is OK.

- I just wanted to make sure that you received my email about the ...
- I just wondered what you think about our offer.
- If you need any further information or have any questions about the proposal, please don't hesitate to give me ring.
- Could you just confirm that you received everything?

General follow-up calls (Keeping in contact)

Sometimes you may wish to call clients and potential clients (also called "leads" or "prospects") just to keep in contact with them. Such follow-up or courtesy calls are quite common in English-speaking countries. Here are some useful phrases for doing this:

- It's quite a few weeks since we last spoke and I just wondered how things are at Daventry Electrics.
- It's a long time since we had contact with one another. I just wanted to enquire about ...
- I thought I would give you a call to check how things are.
- This is just a short courtesy call to check everything is OK.

Example

H: Good afternoon, my name is Thomas Hammerschmidt from WRT Logistics in Frankfurt. I was given your name by a business associate of mine, Dieter Riesenfeld. He told me that you may be looking for a new European supplier in the area of logistics and recommended that I gave you a call. We provide comprehensive services throughout Europe and I wondered whether we could be of potential service to you?

R: I see. Actually, the contract will be going out to competitive tender next month; but since you know Dieter, perhaps you would like to come and tell us what you can do for us?

H: We'd be delighted to do that. When would be the most convenient time for you Mr Roberts?

R: I'm away on business all next week, but anytime the week after next would be fine ...

Calling someone who has been recommended to you

Many business contacts come through "networking" with people. Someone may have given you the name and telephone number of a personal business associate or contact and you need to call them. Making use of personal contacts can be very effective way of doing business. Here are some typical expressions:

- I was given your name by ...
- Your were recommended to me by ...
- Dieter Riesenfeld suggested that I gave you a call because ...
- I understand from Dieter Riesenfeld that you may be looking for ...

Useful vocabulary:

a written quotation:	schriftliches Angebot
bear with someone:	Geduld mit jemandem haben
I just wondered if ... :	Ich wollte nur wissen, ob
lead / prospect:	potenzieller Kunde
business associate:	Geschäftspartner
competitive tender:	Ausschreibung

The angry customer – "sorry" is not enough

What do you do when a customer is angry or very annoyed? Whether it's your company's fault or not: in the USA and Britain "the customer is king (or queen)!" and it's important to show this. Simply saying "sorry" is not always sufficient. As illustrated in the following example, using the word too many times can actually make the situation worse:

Example

C: Sorry? If someone says "sorry" to me once more, I'm going to explode! I expect more than just sorry – what are you doing to put things right?

D: Mr Smith, I can fully understand your frustration. Please rest assured that we are doing everything possible to sort the problem out. As soon as I have any further news, I will let you know.

Some different ways of saying "sorry"

Here are some ways of saying sorry, including expressions that do not involve the word "sorry". Sometimes it's better to use these instead. The greater the number of asterisks, the greater the strength of your apology:

*	I'm sorry for ...
**	I'm very sorry for the error / mistake.
***	I can only apologise for this situation.
***	I'm really sorry about the mistake.

We're very sorry indeed for the inconvenience caused.

**** I'm terribly sorry for the problems you have experienced.

***** I can't apologise enough for the inconvenience caused on this particular occasion. We're doing everything we can to put things right as soon as possible.

Offering compensation

When things go wrong, it is sometimes necessary to offer customers some form of compensation for the inconvenience caused. For example, this could be a discount, partial refund or even a full refund.

Examples

I can appreciate your frustration and disappointment on this occasion. This should not have happened and I can only apologise once again for the inconvenience. As a gesture of good will, I would like to offer you ....

Please accept our apologies for this error. I'll make sure that the correct items are sent to you as soon as possible.

- As a gesture of good will, I would like to offer a 20% discount. I hope that this will help restore your confidence in us.
- By way of compensation for the problems you experienced, we would like to offer ...

- In view of the problems you experienced, we would like to offer you ...
- In view of the inconvenience caused, we are prepared to offer you a 10% discount on your next order.
- As a small gesture of goodwill, we will not be charging for the ...
- In view of the circumstances, I would like to offer you a complimentary meal in our hotel restaurant.

Useful vocabulary:

annoy:	ärgern
discount:	Rabatt, Preisnachlass
refund:	Rückerstattung
appreciate someone's frustration:	verstehen, dass jemand frustriert ist
restore confidence:	Vertrauen wiederherstellen
charge for something	etwas berechnen

How to say "no" politely

In comparison to German, English is often very indirect and saying "no" directly can often offend the other person. To say "no" and not offer any alternative solution is considered highly confrontational. English speakers have many different ways of expressing their opposition to something or giving a negative response. Even when someone asks a closed "yes" or "no" question, it is usual to give a more detailed reply if you are saying no to something. Here are some examples:

Example

Unavailable Service

A: I would like to take out the 6-month service contract at your special introductory rate.

B: I'm terribly sorry Mr Johnson; this offer was for a limited period only and unfortunately is no longer available. In view of the misunderstanding, we could, however, offer you a 10% discount on our normal 12-month service contract, which still represents excellent value and gives you a longer period of cover.

Refund

A: Please can I have a full refund?

B: I'm very sorry, but I'm afraid it is not possible. However, we are prepared to offer a 25% discount on the price. I hope that this will help restore your confidence in us.

Replacement Parts

A: I need the parts tomorrow; you'll have to send them today!

B: Mr Smith, I appreciate your problem, but unfortunately I don't have any way of getting them to you for tomorrow morning. It's too late to arrange a courier today, but I'll make sure they are sent first thing tomorrow morning.

How to avoid just saying "no"

English speakers avoid direct negativity. Very often this is achieved by apologising for it and automatically offering an alternative solution (where possible). Here are several ways of answering the following question:

Do you take credit cards?

– I'm afraid not. However, we would be pleased to accept payment by bankcard or bank transfer.

- I'm sorry but we don't. Is it possible for you to make a bank transfer?
- Unfortunately not. You can however pay by bankcard or direct transfer.
- I'm sorry, but we don't accept them. Would you be able to make a bank transfer?

How to complain successfully

Sometimes things go wrong! Your company has purchased something that is faulty and does not work properly, or you have ordered something that has not yet been delivered. Finding the right "tone" is important to ensure a successful outcome. Remaining courteous and polite is generally more effective and therefore polite forms of verbs (like "could" and "would") are also used.

Example: An outstanding order

I'm calling about an order we made with you last month for ... The goods have still not been delivered and I would like to know when they will be sent. It's now six weeks since we faxed you the order form and we have heard nothing from you since! If I give you the order number, please could you check this for me?

Chasing an order

- Please can you let me know what's happening?
- Could you tell me when I can expect to receive the order?
- What's the current status of the order?

- When will the goods be delivered?
- Can you give me an update on the delivery status please?

Getting something replaced or repaired

Example: Faulty goods

We purchased a new printer from you last week but unfortunately it is faulty. How can we get things put right as quickly as possible? How soon can you send a replacement?

- We need a replacement as soon as possible.
- How soon can you come and fix it?
- Please can you tell me when you will be sending an engineer?
- When will it be repaired?
- How long will it take to repair it?

How good is the service?

Because of the importance of customer service, there are lots of ways to describe it. Companies regularly conduct market research to find out what customers think of their level of customer service.

Example: Poor service

Good afternoon, I'd like to speak to the call centre manager please. I've been trying to get through to one of your service engineers for 2 days but the line is either always busy or there is no reply. It's now really urgent and I need to speak to someone who can help me with this problem.

Here are a range of expressions you can use to talk about the quality of service:

↑↑↑↑↑	The level of service was exceptional!
↑↑↑↑	The service is first-class.
	The service is excellent / really good.
↑↑↑	The standard of service was good.
↑↑	The service was fine.
	They offer an acceptable level of service.
↑	They provide a basic level of service.
↓	Customer service is poor.
↓↓	The service provided was not good at all.
↓↓↓	Their customer service is very poor.
↓↓↓↓	The level of service on this occasion was really bad.
↓↓↓↓↓	The standard of service provided is appalling!

Getting to speak to someone in authority

Using polite forms of the verb, as shown in the following examples, will generally be more effective than simply demanding to speak to the manager.

- I'd like to speak to the office manager please.
- Please could you put me through to your supervisor?
- I would like to speak to the person who is responsible for customer care.
- Could I speak to the person in charge please?

Useful vocabulary:

purchase something:	etwas kaufen
chase an order:	einer Bestellung nachgehen/ eine Bestellung weiterverfolgen
get things put right:	etwas in Ordnung bringen lassen
level of service:	Qualität des Kundendienstes
someone in authority:	jemand mit Entscheidungskompetenz
person in charge:	Verantwortliche(r)

Giving ultimatums and setting deadlines

When doing business, it's sometimes necessary to give people ultimatums (final demands, final offers, final proposals etc.) and set deadlines (a time limit for an activity). It's very important to make sure that these are clear and unambiguous. Making your requirements and expectations clear can avoid unnecessary problems later on. Note the use of the prepositions "by" (*not: until*) and "within" in the following examples.

Examples

I'm very sorry, but unless we receive your written confirmation and deposit by the end of the week, we will have to cancel your provisional order. As I'm sure you will appreciate, we are unable to reserve the items for you indefinitely.

Unless we receive payment within 7 days, we will have no alternative but to take legal action.

If we do not hear from you by Friday 15 June, we will assume that you do not wish to be included in the next edition of the Web Designers Year Book.

Please can you let me know whether you will be attending the meeting by Thursday afternoon at the very latest. If you are unable to come, please arrange for someone to attend in your place.

How urgent is it?

This table gives you a range of expressions in spoken English, depending on the urgency of the situation:

Purpose	Expression
Setting a specific deadline	▪ Please let me know by Thursday next week at the very latest.
You expect a response, but set no deadline	▪ I look forward to hearing from you soon.
It's quite urgent	▪ Please can you let me have the figures as soon as possible?
It's very urgent	▪ Please let me have your report as a matter or urgency.
Immediately	▪ I need your figures now!
An ultimatum	▪ If we don't hear from you by the end of the week, we will assume you no longer require the reservation.
	▪ Unless we receive your confirmation by ...

Useful vocabulary:

by the end of the week / by Friday, 15 June:	bis spätestens Ende der Woche / bis Freitag, 15. Juni
provisional order	vorläufige Bestellung
reserve the items:	Posten / Waren reservieren
within 7 days:	innerhalb von 7 Tagen
take legal action:	den Rechtsweg beschreiten
at the very latest:	spätestens
let someone have something:	jemandem etwas zukommen lassen

Social Situations

Many business activities also involve social situations, for example, a formal business dinner, entertaining clients or socialising with business colleagues after work. English speakers usually make "small talk" on these occasions – light conversation that avoids sensitive issues and respects the privacy of the other person.

This chapter provides you with examples of social situations:

- invitations (page 78) as well as eating and drinking (page 92),
- typical situations and the most common topics for small talk (page 81),
- talking about hobbies and interests (page 88) as well as about your company and your job (page 90).

Invitations

Invitations to socialise with colleagues after work or even at weekends are sometimes just as important in business as formal invitations to business lunches or dinners. The way we make and accept /decline such invitations is also very important, particularly when making a first impression. If you are unable (or even do not want to) accept it, make sure you decline an invitation in the politest way possible. This generally means expressing your regret that you cannot make it.

Example

A: If you have time, I wonder if you would like to join us for dinner this evening: I know a good local fish restaurant and it would be a good opportunity to talk informally about the project.

B: That's very kind of you, but unfortunately I have another business engagement this evening. Perhaps we could get together tomorrow evening?

A: I'm terribly sorry, but I already have another appointment on Wednesday evening. What about lunch?

B: That would be fine. I've got a meeting with your Finance Director at eleven, but that should only take about an hour.

A: Great! Shall we say twelve-thirty then? I'll call by and pick you up after your meeting.

How to accept an invitation

Would you like to join us for a drink after work?

- Thank you very much. That would be lovely.
- Yes, that sounds a great idea. Thanks for inviting me.
- I'd love to. I can't wait to try some real English beer!

How to decline an invitation politely

Would you like to join us for a meal on Wednesday evening?

- I'd love to come, but unfortunately I already have another engagement that evening.
- I really appreciate you asking me, but I'm sorry to say I have to leave for the airport directly after the meeting.
- Thanks very much for the invitation but unfortunately I can't make it this time.
- Thanks very much for inviting me but I'll have to say no this time. Hopefully on another occasion ...

Thanking someone at the end or afterwards

- Thank you very much for the lovely evening, I really enjoyed it!
- Thank you for your hospitality. It was so kind of you to invite me to dinner at your house.
- Thanks for arranging the meal and booking the restaurant: it was a great evening!
- It was a great evening, I really enjoyed it!
- Thank you very much for the nice evening.

> An invitation – but who pays?
> The word "invitation" or the verb "to invite" in English does not have the same financial implications as the German equivalent. When someone "invites" you to join them, for example, in a bar or pub after work, it does not automatically mean that they are going to pay!
> But if a business colleague "invites" you to join him/her for a formal or official business dinner then, like in German, they are also indicating that

they will pay. However, when a colleague says to you "A group of us are going to a pizza place after work and we would like to invite you to join us", it is most likely that everyone will pay for their own meal! However, expect the bill to be presented for the entire table: Settling the bill individually is not normal in English-speaking countries. The group will then have to split the amount between them. When everyone has consumed a similar amount of food and drink, simply dividing the total bill by the number of people present is common and sometimes saves a lot of time!

When you would like to pay the bill

Indicating that you would like to pay for someone is often done at the time the bill arrives. Here are some useful phrases:

- Let me get this.
- This one's on me / us.
- You're our guest, please let me settle this.
- That's very kind of you, but I'd like to pay for the meal if you don't mind.

Useful vocabulary:

have a previous engagement:	etwas vorhaben
call by:	vorbeischauen
appreciate:	schätzen
hospitality:	Gastfreundlichkeit

Small talk

Small talk is important in business as well as for socialising. For example, at the beginning of a phone call you should engage in a little small talk. Talking business immediately is considered unfriendly. An important aspect of small talk is being able to ask people questions about themselves. English speakers are often happy to talk about their personal experiences and feelings, but will normally wait until they are asked to do so. Be prepared to ask lots of questions! This does not mean having to talk about personal things if you do not want to; but do be prepared to reveal some of your own interests, likes, dislikes and ambitions if and when asked.

Small talk is light conversation for social occasions and is very important to English speakers. Ask "open" questions like the ones below, to indicate your interest in the person you are talking to. Avoid talking too much about yourself and expressing your own opinion too often. Religion, politics and other very personal topics are best avoided, unless you know the person/people very well! English speakers may ask more personal questions about you and your family than you are used to, for example about the area where you live and what type of house or apartment you have.

Some of the most common topics for small talk

Talking about the weather

Making small talk about the weather is very common in all English-speaking countries, particularly in Britain where complaining about the weather is almost a national pastime.

Example

A: I suppose you find Hamburg rather cold and wet in comparison to Houston?

B: Yes, it is a bit of a shock but I don't miss the humidity. The fresh breeze is really great here and I can sleep in my hotel without running the air conditioning.

A: What sort of temperatures do you have in Houston at this time of year then?

B: It's normally around eighty-five (degrees) and very sticky. You sort of get used to it! We tend to drive everywhere because of the heat.

A: People here complain about the wind and rain, but we still enjoy eating outdoors and cycling around the city. Have you seen the Alster yet?

B: No, not yet. I plan to do some sightseeing on Saturday.

Comparing places

- Hamburg is wetter than Barcelona.
- The winters in New York are colder than in London.
- Brisbane is sunnier than Hanover.
- Los Angeles is a lot warmer than Stockholm.
- The evenings in Munich are cooler than in Frankfurt.
- The temperatures in Moscow are more extreme than in Paris.

What sports are you interested in?

Although it's not everyone's "cup of tea", talking about sports is a very popular topic for small talk. Whether you follow sports just as a spectator or are a passionate amateur athlete – be prepared to talk about it!

Example

A: Have you been watching any of the world championships on TV? Are you pleased with the performance of the Australian team?

B: To tell you the truth, I haven't had a chance to watch any of it so far. Have we been doing badly then?

A: No, the Australians have been doing rather well. I think you've won more medals than any other country. How come Australian swimmers are so good?

B: Sports are very important in Australia, particularly in school, where all kids are encouraged to take part in as many different sports activities as possible. It's almost a national obsession!

- I'm very interested in athletics.
- He's keen on all kinds of winter sports.
- I support our local football team.
- I follow the Italian League and watch most games on TV.
- She takes a great interest in tennis, particularly the grand slam tournaments.
- I compete in local swimming championships and train several times a week.

Talking about travel

Example

A: Is this your first visit to Düsseldorf?

B: Yes it is. I was also in Berlin two years ago but it was a very short visit and I didn't have time for sightseeing.

A: That's a shame! Berlin is a great city with lots to see and do. I prefer Düsseldorf of course because it's my home!

B: Have you ever been to Hong Kong?

A: No, not yet. It's one of the places I want to visit. I love travelling, particularly in Asia. When's the best time to visit?

B: Oh, you should come in early spring or autumn when it's not so hot and humid. I would be happy to show you around if you do come.

A: That's very kind of you. I hope I'll be able to take you up on that one day! Have you seen anything of Düsseldorf yet?

B: No not yet. I hope to spend some time looking around on Friday, before going to the airport.

A: If you would like to give me a call in the morning, I can give you a quick tour of the city if you like.

B: That would be great! I'll call you as soon as the meeting has finished.

- They love France and go there every year.
- He prefers backpacking on his own.
- I don't like long-haul flights and usually choose a holiday destination fairly close to home.
- We always go to Italy by car. It's a long drive, but the scenery is fantastic.
- We go skiing every year at the same resort. We've been going there for years. It's still more or less unspoilt and the scenery is fantastic. We've always had good snow.
- Places and countries you have visited or would like to visit:
  - Have you ever been to New York?
  - I haven't been to Portugal yet, but it's on my list of places to visit.
  - I've never been to Beijing. How did you find it?
  - Did you go to South America on business or was it vacation?

When talking about Germany, English speakers refer to: The Baltic Coast / Sea (*not: the "East Coast or Sea"!*) and the North Sea.

European countries, people and languages

When talking about countries, the people who live there and the languages spoken in them, it's important to use the correct terms. Mistakes could cause embarrassment and even offence! The following table will probably contain a few surprises:

Country	Inhabitant(s)	Language
Belgium	Belgian(s)	French, Flemish, German
Croatia	Croat(s), Croatian(s)	Croatian
Cyprus	Cypriot(s)	Greek, Turkish
Czech Republic	Czech(s)	Czech
Denmark	Dane(s)	Danish
England	English	English
Estonia	Estonian(s)	Estonian
Finland	Finn(s)	Finnish
France	French	French
Greece	Greek(s)	Greek
Hungary	Hungarian(s)	Hungarian

Ireland	Irish	Irish (Gaelic), English,
Latvia	Latvian(s)	Latvian (also known as Lettish)
Lithuania	Lithuanian(s)	Lithuanian
Luxembourg	Luxembourger	French, German, Luxemburgish
Malta	Maltese	Maltese, English
Netherlands	Dutch	Dutch
Norway	Norwegian(s)	Norwegian
Poland	Pole(s)	Polish
Portugal	Portuguese	Portuguese
Russia	Russian(s)	Russian
Scotland	Scot(s)	Scottish Gaelic, English
Slovenia	Slovenian(s)	Slovene
Slovakia	Slovakian(s)	Slovak
Sweden	Swede(s)	Swedish
Switzerland	Swiss	German, French, Italian, Romansch
Turkey	Turk(s)	Turkish
Wales	Welsh	Welsh, English

Likes and dislikes in respect of food and drink

Example

A: What do you think of German food then? Have you tried some of our Bavarian specialities yet?

B: I'm not sure if they were Bavarian, but I did have some rather good sausages last night in the hotel restaurant. What else do you recommend I should try?

A: Bavaria is very famous for its beer of course – best enjoyed in one of our many beer gardens on a warm summer's evening. Dumplings are another German speciality – there are various types made from bread, potato or even semolina. Bavarian dumplings are normally made from bread.

B: What do you normally eat with them?

A: Traditionally we serve pork or other roast meat with them and red cabbage.

- I'm not so keen on rice.
- I prefer fish grilled rather than fried; the flavour is much better.
- Do you have any particular dislikes – I mean is there anything that you don't eat?
- I have a nut allergy and try to avoid eating anything containing nuts or nut products.
- I drink both red and white wine: Do you have a particular preference?
- I eat almost anything – there's not much I don't like!
- I love fish, particularly fresh salmon.
- I try to eat low-fat food.

Starting small talk

It's important to be able to start small talk. This is a skill that often requires practice. Try to use open questions that require more than just a "yes" or "no" answer to get other people talking. Here are some phrases you can use when you have foreign visitors, or when you are away on business:

- What do you think of Berlin?
- How do you find the food?
- How are you enjoying your visit to ...
- What's your impression of Germany?
- What do you think of the wine / beer / food etc?
- What's your hotel like?
- Do you have anything like this in Vancouver?
- How was your flight?
- What was your journey like?
- How does this bar / restaurant compare to the ones in Sydney?

Hobbies and interests

Talking about your hobbies and interests is an important part of making small talk. People will think you are boring if you just talk about your work and are generally flattered if you ask them about their interests. Finding a topic of common interest can help break the ice at social functions.

What do you do in your spare time? / Do you have any particular hobbies or interests?

- I enjoy...
  - swimming / playing football / cycling / inline skating / jogging / skiing.
  - cooking / reading / gardening / playing the piano / singing / dancing / travelling / going to the cinema / going to the theatre and opera.
- I spend as much time as I can with my children.
- I am chairperson of the local residents' association.
- I like listening to jazz.
- I listen to a lot of classical music.
- I'm quite a D.I.Y. enthusiast and enjoy painting and decorating.

> D.I.Y. ("do-it-yourself") – the activity of repairing or making things, particularly at home can also be a hobby.

Answering a question with another question

Other sections of this book have already referred to the importance of politeness in English-speaking countries. One essential element of this politeness is to show an interest in the person you are talking to. Since people tend to ask questions about things that are of interest to them, once you have given your own answer, it's a good idea to ask them what they think about the same topic. Here are some expressions you can use after you have answered a particular question:

- And what about you?
- And yourself?
- And you? Do you have any particular hobbies?
- How about you?

Talking about your company and job

Basic introductions were covered in Chapter 1 (see page 8). Not everyone is interested in your job, so be careful to avoid long monologues. Asking additional questions is a good way of showing interest. Here are some more examples of people making small talk about their jobs:

Example

A: I suppose your job must involve a lot or travelling?

B: Yes it does. I'm on the road at least two or three days a week. Most of my customers are in Germany, but I also look after Holland, Belgium and Luxembourg.

A: I imagine it must get quite tedious living out of hotels?

B: You get used to it. I try and organise my diary so that I'm always working from my home office on Fridays. What about you?

A: Oh, apart from the occasional conference and trade fair, I'm based in the office. Being based at headquarters means that most colleagues from the field come to us!

Expressing understanding

People want to be understood. That is, after all, one of the main aims of good communication. Giving a person the feeling that you understand their problems is an excellent way to build bridges and build a relationship. In business conversations and the accompanying small talk it is, of course, wise to concentrate on the good job that they do and the difficult circumstances that they have to deal with. Here are some useful phrases:

- I suppose you spend a lot of time on aircraft?
- I imagine you must have seen a lot of European cities by now?
- I bet it's really hectic for you in the summer.
- You must have a very large workload.
- And are you in charge of the entire project?
- Your job obviously requires good organisational skills.
- I guess you are very busy preparing for ...

Example

A: I notice that your company has a fairly informal dress code. Is that just in the Kiel office?

B: No, it's a companywide thing. It comes from our parent company in the US, where everyone "dresses down" for the weekend on Fridays. Even the Vice President wears jeans and a polo shirt!

A: I think that's a great idea. We still have a very formal dress code – no jeans or t-shirts what ever day of the week it is. The British still have a very conservative attitude with regard to what is acceptable in the office.

Referring to observations

Talking about something you have noticed indicates your interest in a particular situation or person. The following phrases are used to talk about things you have seen or observed:

– I notice that most people in the office drive to work. Does the company provide free parking?
– I noticed your new company logo. When did you introduce it?
– I saw a lot of people out shopping last night. Are the shops open late every night of the week?
– I find the people in the hotel really friendly. Do you use this hotel because of its good service?

Useful vocabulary:

be flattered:	sich geschmeichelt fühlen
D.I.Y. enthusiast:	Heimwerker
football enthusiast:	Fußballfan
theatre enthusiast:	Theaterliebhaber
workload:	Arbeitspensum / Arbeitsbelastung
in charge of the project:	für das Projekt verantwortlich
fairly:	ziemlich
parent company:	Muttergesellschaft

Eating and drinking

Doing business often involves eating and drinking with colleagues both formally (business dinners, conferences etc.) and informally (celebrating birthdays, socialising with colleagues etc.). The following section includes some useful phrases and examples.

Booking or arriving at a restaurant

- I'd like to reserve a table for six people for eight thirty.
- Do you have a table for four please?
- We'd like a non-smoking table please.
- Are you fully licensed? (*Meaning: Do you serve alcohol? See box below.*)
- Is the restaurant air-conditioned?
- Do you have car parking?
- I've never been before: Could you give me directions please?

> Some smaller restaurants in many English-speaking areas of the world (United Kingdom, New Zealand, Australia and North America) are unlicensed and do not sell alcohol. Many of these restaurants allow you to take your own wine or beer, often indicated by the letters "BYO" (bring your own), which you can consume in the restaurant for a small service charge (known as "corkage").

Example

A: I'm afraid they've only got menus in German here. Would you like me to tell you what everything is?

B: Yes please, that would be really helpful. I did learn a little German in school, but that's quite a few years ago now. Can you recommend any local specialities?

A: Let's see ... The venison dishes are always very good and the meat is all from local farms. Then of course there's always the sausages ...

Specific kinds of food and drink

- Are there any vegetarian dishes on the menu today?
- What local specialities do you recommend?
- It is possible to have rice instead of potatoes with the main course?
- Do they serve wine by the glass as well as by the bottle?
- Is there a set lunch menu or is it "à la carte"?
- Can you recommend a good wine to have with the beef?

Talking about what you are going to order

Any meal will involve some discussion with your fellow guests about the menu and what you're going to order.

Example

A: Do you know what you're going to order yet?

B: I'm not quite sure. I'm very tempted by the duck, but the lamb also sounds delicious. What about you?

A: Oh, I'm going to have spaghetti with seafood. It's my favourite!

- Have you made up your mind yet? / Do you know what you're going to have yet?
- Yes, I'm going to have the ... What about you?
- I'm tempted by the ...
- I'm not sure whether to have the .... or the ...

NEU

Strategien und Taktiken

e book | Buch

978-3-648-02555-0
€ 8,95 [D], € 9,30 [A], sFr 10,95

→ Wie Sie Verhandlungen vorbereiten und geschickt ins Thema einsteigen.
→ Wie Sie Stress abbauen und eine angenehme Situation schaffen.
→ Wie Sie aus festgefahrenen Situationen herausfinden.

Richtig auftreten

- Wie Sie Hemmungen überwinden und den passenden Gesprächseinstieg finden.
- Welche Themen und Techniken Sie nutzen können.
- Wie Sie schwierige Situationen souverän meistern.

Buch 978-3-448-09087-1
€ 6,90 [D], € 7,10 [A], sFr 8,95

- Welche Signale Sie unbewusst durch Körperhaltung, Gestik und Stimme transportieren.
- Wie Sie die Botschaften anderer richtig interpretieren und selbst überzeugen.
- Körpersprache in Vorstellungsgesprächen und Meetings gezielt einsetzen.

Buch 978-3-648-02683-0
€ 8,95 [D], € 9,30 [A], sFr 10,95

Alles im Griff haben

- Die eigenen Interessen verwirklichen – mit dem richtigen Auftreten.
- Souverän verhandeln und argumentieren – Gesprächsstrategien für jede Situation.
- Selbstdarstellung und Netzwerke – wie Sie sich selbst besser vermarkten.

Buch 978-3-448-09100-7
€ 6,90 [D], € 7,10 [A], sFr 8,95

- Typische Manipulationstechniken und elegante Abwehrtechniken.
- Argumentationsfallen und Scheinargumente durchschauen und entkräftigen.
- Mit großem Trainingsteil: erkennen, entlarven, kontern. Auch in heiklen Situationen.

e-book Buch 978-3-648-02685-4
€ 8,95 [D], € 9,30 [A], sFr 10,95

Fit im Beruf

Buch 978-3-648-00311-4
€ 6,90 [D], € 7,10 [A], sFr 8,95

Buch 978-3-648-00312-1
€ 6,90 [D], € 7,10 [A], sFr 8,95

Buch 978-3-648-02721-9
€ 8,95 [D], € 9,30 [A], sFr 10,95

Buch 978-3-648-02723-3
€ 8,95 [D], € 9,30 [A], sFr 10,95

Rechnungswesen leicht gemacht

- Inventur, Bilanz, Konto-Begriffe und Zusammenhänge verständlich erklärt – von der Inventur über die Bilanz zum Konto.
- Exemplarische Buchungen aus der täglichen Praxis: Debitoren, Kreditoren, Steuern u. v. m.
- Alle wichtigen Geschäftsvorfälle aus der Praxis kennen und korrekt buchen.

Buch
978-3-448-09303-2
€ 6,90 [D], € 7,10 [A], sFr 8,95

- Schnell finden und korrekt anwenden - die wichtigsten Kennzahlen und Formeln.
- Beschaffung und Investitionsrechnung, Fertigung und Kostenrechnung, Bilanzkennzahlen und Finanzierung.
- Mit großem Praxisteil: die wichtigsten Fragen für Unternehmensentscheidungen und ihre Lösung.

Buch
978-3-648-00492-0
€ 6,90 [D], € 7,10 [A], sFr 8,95

NEU

Einfach nachschlagen

- Wachstum, Wettbewerb und Arbeit verständlich erklärt.
- Thema Geld: Warum Inflation schädlich ist und für wen.
- Fallbeispiele und Erläuterungen zu statistischen Untersuchungen.

e book | Buch
978-3-648-02552-9
€ 8,95 [D], € 9,30 [A], sFr 10,95

- Was sich hinter den englischen Fachtermini im Wirtschaftssektor verbirgt: *das* Nachschlagewerk von A-Z!
- Die wichtigsten Fachausdrücke aus Bank- und Börsenwelt, Management und Wirtschaftspolitik, Investor Relations und Corporate Governance.

e book | Buch
978-3-648-02550-5
€ 8,95 [D], € 9,30 [A], sFr 10,95

Ordering meals

Example

W: Would you like to order now?

A: Yes we would. I'd like the risotto as a starter, followed by the roast duck. Does it come with vegetables?

W: Yes it does. Today's vegetables are garden peas, fresh baby courgettes and new potatoes.

B: I would like the asparagus soup to start; followed by the risotto as a main course. I'd also like a small side salad.

W: Fine. What would you like to drink with your meal?

A: I'll have a glass of the house white please.

B: And for me, the house red.

...

W: Would you like to see our dessert menu? ...

A: I'm very tempted by the treacle tart. Is it possible to have it with ice-cream instead of custard?

W: Yes of course. Would you like coffee as well?

A: No, not at the moment thanks. I think we'll wait until after the pudding.

B: And I'd just like the fruit salad on its own please – no cream or ice-cream.

- I would like the prawn cocktail to start with and then the grilled trout.
- I'd just like roast lamb as a main course. No starter thank you.
- As a starter, I'd like the deep fried mushrooms please, followed by the vegetarian lasagne with a green salad.
- We'd also like a bottle of the house red please.

Paying

It is common in all English-speaking countries to issue one bill per table. Any splitting of the amount is left to the guests themselves.

- Could we have the bill (*US*: check) please? Is it possible to pay by credit card?)
- Please can you bring the bill? Is it possible to put the drinks on a separate account?
- Can you charge this to my room please – it's 316.
- We're splitting the bill between us. Please can you charge 25 pounds to each credit card?

Further information about paying the bill in restaurants can be found in the section dealing with invitations on page 78.

Useful vocabulary:

give someone directions:	jemandem eine Wegbeschreibung geben
fellow guests:	die anderen Gäste
make up one's mind:	sich entscheiden
be tempted by something:	etwas verlockend finden *Wenn es ums Essen geht, z.B: "Der Fisch klingt total lecker."*
starter:	Vorspeise
issue one bill per table:	eine Rechung pro Tisch ausstellen
charge something to the room:	etwas aufs Zimmer schreiben (lassen)

Written Communication

Written communication will also influence your business success. It's important to make sure everything is as correct as possible.

This chapter provides

- a brief guide to writing emails, letters, agendas and minutes for meetings (page 98).
- It also gives you some useful phrases for starting and finishing your text (page 105).

Emails

A lot of business emails in English are not only very informal but also very badly written: Sentences are often incomplete and the grammar incorrect! This makes it very difficult for you as a non-native speaker. Emails should, however, be treated like any other piece of written communication, with attention to grammar, punctuation and style.

Formal or informal?

The following examples show some formal and informal styles:

Examples

Very Formal

Dear Mr Stephens,

I refer to your email from 25 February and thank you for your enquiry. We would be delighted to provide the services you require for the Frankfurt Book Fair. Please find attached a quotation, which I trust will be acceptable to you.

Should you require any further information, please do not hesitate to contact us. I look forward to hearing from you in due course.

Yours sincerely,

Michael Landmesser
Sales Director
GHW Marketing GmbH

Fairly Formal

Dear Andrew,

Thank you for your email from 25 February enquiring about services for the Frankfurt Book Fair. I hope that the attached quotation is acceptable to you.

If you require any further information please do not hesitate to contact us. I look forward to hearing from you.

With best regards,

Michael Landmesser
Sales Director
GHW Marketing GmbH

Informal

Hallo Andrew,

Thank you for your email from 25 February enquiring about the Frankfurt Book Fair. We would be pleased to provide the services you require. Our quotation is attached – I hope you will find it acceptable.

If you need any other information, please let us know. I look forward to hearing from you.

Best regards,

Michael Landmesser
Sales Director
GHW Marketing GmbH

Very Informal

Hi Andy!

Thanks for your email of 25 February. We would be very pleased to provide the services you require for the Frankfurt Book Fair. Please find attached quotation, which I hope you will find OK.

Please let me know if you need anything else.

Kind regards,

Michael

How do I know whether to use formal or informal language? Finding the right tone and level of formality for an email is sometimes difficult. If in doubt, use formal English. Grammar and punctuation should be correct in all business emails. You should always use lower and upper case letters as appropriate. However, you may not always receive emails that are correctly written and in good business English! The use of slang and over friendly expressions should be avoided unless you are really sure that it is OK to use them. If in doubt, exercise caution and be conservative.

Abbreviations

The use of abbreviations is very common in emails. A list of the most common standard abbreviations in English can be found in the Appendix on page 115. Using abbreviations saves time and space, but only use expressions that you are sure the recipient of the email will understand! Take a look at the following text written with and without abbreviations:

Example

Dear Angela,

Thank you for your email of 17 December.

For your information, I am attaching a full programme for the event. If you need accommodation next month, please let me know as soon as possible.

I will be at Headquarters on Monday (arriving around 10.30 hours). Perhaps we could meet for lunch?

With kind regards,

Günter

PS: Please give my best regards to Roger and everyone in the Operations Department!

Dear Angela,

Tks for yr email of 17 Dec.

FYI: I am attaching a full programme for the event. If you need accommodation for next month, pls let me know ASAP.

I will be at HQ on Mon. (arr. ca. 10.30 hrs). Perhaps we cld meet for lunch?

Kind rgds,

Günter

PS: Pls give my best regards to Roger and everyone in the Ops. Dept.!

Text messages

"Texting" (sending and receiving messages via mobile phone) is useful in certain circumstances to convey important business information. In order to use as few characters as possible, special abbreviations and unique expressions have developed. More of these are given in the Appendix on page 115.

Examples

ARR 19:30 FLT BA902. CU AT HOTEL. RGDS MARIAN (Arriving 19.30 hours with flight BA902. See you at the hotel. Regards, Marian)

TKS 4 YR MSG. PLS CALL ASAP WHEN U ARR AT APT. TKS ROBERT (Thanks for your message. Please call as soon as possible when you arrive at the airport. Thanks, Robert)

SRY, HAVE BKD A TABLE FOR 8PM. SPK 2 U L8R (Sorry, I have booked a table for 8.00 PM. Speak to you later)

Some terms and abbreviations for texting in English

OTOH	On the other hand
BTW	By the way
CID	Consider it done
AFAIK	As far as I know
THX / TX	Thank you
PCM	Please call me
PLS	Please
RGDS	Regards
SRY	Sorry

The German word "Handy" is not used in English-speaking countries. In Britain people use mobile phones (often just referred to as a "mobile") and in America cell phones. Although the term SMS (short message service) is English, the expression is not used: English speakers send text messages ("text") and spend a lot of time texting other people.

Letters

There are several important differences between letters in German and English:

- The subject line comes after the greeting / salutation in British English, but before it in US English.
- Begin the main text (body) of the letter with an upper case letter, even though it follows the "comma" after the greeting.
- The complimentary close will vary depending whether you are writing to someone personally (Dear Mr ..., Mrs ...) by name or impersonally (Dear Sir or Madam).
- In the signature line give your name, job title and then, if necessary, the company name. However, your company may have its own policy on the layout of the signature line.

Examples

Dear Sir or Madam,

Visitor Information

I will be visiting Bath next month on business and would be grateful if you could send me information about hotels, local business organisations and details of evening events and possible things to do.

Yours faithfully,

Peter Stein

Dear Ms Hatful,

Your Visit to Essen on 25 May

Further to our telephone conversation today, I have pleasure in enclosing some information about our company and the local area. Details of your hotel accommodation and the full itinerary for the visit will be sent to you directly by our personnel department in the next few days.

If I can be of any further assistance in the meantime, please do not hesitate to contact me.

I look forward to meeting you personally on the 25th of May.

Yours sincerely,

Torsten Haverstock
Business Development Manager

Enc.

Dear Mike,

Supplier Registration

We are currently setting up a new supplier database and are in the process of collecting additional information from all our existing suppliers. I would be grateful therefore if you could complete and return the enclosed supplier registration form to me as soon as possible.

This information will not affect our currently agreed terms and conditions that are valid until 31 December.

Many thanks and best regards,

Hermann Kornhauser
Contracts Manager

Enc.

Choosing the correct form of address

Today, use of 'Ms' in business correspondence has become widespread, as a preferred title which does not focus on whether a woman is married or not. Unlike German, to address someone as "Mrs" in English implies they are married. If you do not know whether someone is married, then always use 'Ms' in any kind of written communication. If a woman's preference is known (i.e. the person concerned has already signed a letter using the term "Mrs"), it is courteous to respect this.

The use of first names in business is very common in English-speaking countries, even in formal business correspondence and meetings. However, first names should only be used if you already know or have met the person concerned.

The contents of a business letter

Here are some standard phrases for beginning and finishing a business letter:

Greeting

You know the name of the person you are writing to:	Dear Mr, Ms, Mrs, Dr Jones,
You do not know who you are writing to:	Dear Sir or Madam,
The person is a close business contact:	Dear John, / Dear Jane,

The finish

If you know the name of the person you are writing to:	Yours sincerely,
If you do not know the name of the person you are writing to. Used mainly in British English:	Yours faithfully,
These are often used in American English:	Sincerely (yours), Yours truly
If the person is a good business contact or friend:	Best regards, With best regards,
These should only be used if the person is also a good personal friend:	Kind regards, Best wishes,

Standard phrases to use in the text

The following phrases are typical of many business letters. They may be useful when formulating your own text.

Reference

- Thank you for your letter of 13 August.
- Further to our telephone conversation today. / yesterday. / last week. / on Friday. / on 26 February.

- Thank you for visiting our stand at the IT Expo in Frankfurt. / your enquiry regarding ...
- With reference to your recent telephone enquiry. / letter of 08 May.

Purpose

- I am writing to enquire about the cost of ...
- Please could you send me a copy of your current brochure. / details of ...
- I am writing to confirm arrangements for our meeting on...

Positive reply

- We would be delighted to be of service to you on this occasion.
- I am pleased to confirm the following: ...

Negative reply

- Unfortunately, we are not able to provide details of the programme. / the event is already fully booked.
- We very much regret to inform you that your application has not been successful on this occasion.

Attachments

- Please find enclosed information about ... / contract.
- We have pleasure in enclosing details of our ...

Closing remarks

- I look forward to hearing from you in due course. / seeing you on 18 July. / meeting you at the conference.
- If I can be of any further assistance, please do not hesitate to contact me.
- We thank you for your custom and look forward to being of service to you again in the future.
- We trust that our offer will be acceptable to you and look forward to receiving your confirmation in due course.
- Should you require any further information at any time, please do not hesitate to contact us.

Written deadlines: How urgent is it?

This table gives you a range of expressions in written English, depending on the urgency of the situation:

Purpose	Expression
Setting a specific deadline for a reply	Please let me have your feedback by Thursday next week at the very latest.
You expect a rely, but set no deadline	I look forward to hearing from you in due course.
It's quite urgent	I would appreciate hearing your views on this as soon as possible.
It's very urgent	Please let me have your input as a matter of urgency.

A deadline and threat to take legal action	Unless we hear from you within seven days, we will be forced to take further (legal) action.
An ultimatum	If we do not hear from you within 14 days, we will cancel the booking.
Immediately	Please submit your application by return.

Compare these phrases with those used in spoken English on pages 75.

Agendas & minutes for meetings

Many meetings require planning and efficient follow-up. A good agenda will help focus on the discussions. The minutes are an important documentation of what was said and agreed.

> The English word "protocol" is a false friend! A general written summary of a meeting is known as "the minutes".

Agendas

Example

Meeting Thursday 23 August, 10.30 hrs
at The Grand Hotel, Norwich
AGENDA
1. Apologies for absence
2. Minutes of the last Meeting held on 22 June (attached)
3. Matters arising from the Minutes.

4. Financial Report
5. Budget 2008/9
6. Marketing issues
7. Dates and venue of future meetings
8. A.O.B.

Before the meeting

- Do you have an agenda for tomorrow's meeting?
- I will send you the agenda by email. Please let me know if I've forgotten anything or if you would like anything added.
- The agenda looks fine, but I think we also need to talk about ...
- The agenda is too long. Perhaps we need to have a separate meeting to discuss next year's budget?
- I'm sorry but I'm unable to come to the meeting next week and wish to give my apologies.
- Who will be chairing the meeting next week?
- Please confirm that you are able to attend or who will be attending in your place.

Minutes

Example

Minutes of the Meeting held on Thursday 25 August at the Grand Hotel, Norwich

Present: Nick Spicer (Chairman), Paul Fisher (minute taker), Malcolm Evans, Mary Jackson, Catherine Piper, Linda Bale.

1. Apologies: Michael O'Connor, Linda Gresham

2. Minutes of the Meeting held on 21 October. Approved.

3. Matters arising from the Minutes.

(i) Ag.3(i.) The HR Director is to follow up on this matter and report back at the next meeting

(ii) Ag.5. The Administration Manager will be speaking to Andrew Jones within the next few days regarding a solution to the parking problems at HQ.

(iii) Ag.6(i). Following the success of the company road shows in September, the Marketing Director indicated his intention to run these again in Jan./Feb.

4. Financial Report.

The Finance Manager reported on the current financial position. This is better than expected due to strong sales during the first half of the year.

5. Budget 2011/12. Advance information was circulated to all present. Full information packs will be sent to all company managers by 30 September (Deadline for completion: 31 October).

6. Marketing Matters. No other marketing matters were discussed under this item.

7. Dates and venue of future meetings.

(i) 18 October at 10.30 hrs – venue to be confirmed

(ii) 15 January at 14.00 hrs at Headquarters (Board Room)

8. A.O.B. None

The meeting ended at 13.15 hours.

After the meeting

- Here are the minutes for last week's meeting. I hope that I have included everything that we discussed.
- Please can you check them and let me have your approval as soon as possible. I will then make sure everyone gets a copy.
- I'm not sure what we finally agreed at the meeting – I'll need to check the minutes!
- Can you let me have a copy of the minutes for my own file?

Appendix

Internet resources

There are many free English language resources available on the Internet, including news and entertainment, as well as specific websites for learning and improving your English. A broadband Internet connection is normally essential for audio and video streams.

> Try listening to or watching the news in English, after you have heard or seen it in German. It's a good way to improve your vocabulary. Also, many films on DVD can be viewed in the original language (often with subtitles) as well as in German. Watch some of your favourite movies again in English!

Internet General	
www.bbc.co.uk	BBC Main Website
http://news.bbc.co.uk	BBC News Website
Internet Radio	
www.bbc.co.uk/radio	Internet radio including BBC World Service and UK stations.
www.bloomberg.com/media/radio	News from New York
www.cbc.ca/programguide/radio	Canadian Broadcasting Co.
www.abc.net.au/newsradio/listen	Australian Broadcasting Co.

Internet Television/Radio	
www.bloomberg.com/media/tv	US, UK and Asia-Pacific
http://itn.co.uk	News headlines, world news and news of Britain
Online Newspapers	
www.nzherald.co.nz	The New Zealand Herald
www.theaustralian.news.com.au	The Australian
http://timesofindia.indiatimes.com	The Times of India
Business Media	
www.economist.com	World business reports and analysis
www.ft.com	International financial and business news

Specific Sites for Learning and Improving English

- http://owad.de (One-Word-A-Day from Paul Smith (vocabulary))
- www.bbc.co.uk/worldservice/learningenglish (BBC Learning English - news articles, video and audio sequences, exercises, newsletter etc.)
- www.learnenglish.org.uk (Website from the British Council with games, quizzes, grammar exercises, e-cards and more)

Dictionaries

- http://dictionary.reverso.net (Translation dictionaries etc.)
- www.thefreedictionary.com (Online dictionaries etc.)

- www.acronymfinder.com (Searchable database of acronyms and abbreviations (incl. English, German and French)
- www.macmillandictionaries.com (Resources section incl. games, dictation and e-lessons)

The Internet addresses given were correct at the time of going to press. The author is not responsible for the contents and availability of these sites.

Common abbreviations

Abbreviation	Meaning	Usage
AKA	also known as	
AOB	any other business	meetings
approx.	approximately	
arr.	arrival	
ASAP	as soon as possible	
attn.	attention	
B2B	business to business	marketing & sales
B2C	business to consumer	marketing & sales
c. / ca.	circa (at the approximate time of)	
canx	cancel	
CEO	chief executive officer	
CET	Central European Time	

cfm.	confirm	
CFO	chief financial officer	
c.o.b.	close of business	deadlines
corp.	corporation	
CU	see you	text messages
dep.	departure	
dept.	department	
e.g.	for example	
enc.	enclosure	
esp.	especially	
Esq.	Esquire	formal title
est.	established	
ETA	expected time of arrival	travel
etc.	et cetera	
FAO	For the attention of	faxes / address labels
FAQ	frequently asked questions	particularly in the Internet
FOC	free of charge	
fwd.	forward	
FYI	for your information	faxes, text messages
GMT	Greenwich Mean Time	see also UTC
HQ	headquarters	

i.e.	that is	
inc.	incorporated (company)	esp. US
incl.	including	
IT	information technology	
K	000 = thousands	85K = eighty-five thousand
Ltd.	Limited (company)	
max.	maximum	
m	metres (also miles)	
MD	managing director	
memo.	memorandum	
mill / M	million	
min.	minimum (also minutes)	
P&P	postage and packaging	
P.S. / PS	postscript	
P.T.O / p.t. o	please turn over	
Pax	people	travel
PLC	public limited company	esp. UK
PLS / pls	please	
PTO	please turn over	
qty.	quantity	
recd.	received	
ref.	reference	

reg.	registered	
RSVP	please reply (to an invitation)	from French
s.a.e	stamped addressed envelope	
SOR	sale or return	
telecom	telephone conversation	
teleconf	telephone conference	
USP	unique selling proposition	marketing & sales
UTC	Universal Time (Coordinated)	see also GMT
VAT / v.a.t	value-added tax	

Numbers

0–99

0	zero(nought, oh)
21	twenty-one
33	thirty-three
47	forty-seven
52	fifty-two
67	sixty-seven
79	seventy-nine
86	eighty-six
94	ninety-four

100 – 1,000,000

1,000	one thousand
2,000	two thousand
10,000	ten thousand
11,759	eleven thousand seven hundred and fifty-nine
20,015	twenty thousand and fifteen
21,000	twenty one thousand
54,000	fifty four thousand
100,000	one hundred thousand
999,000	nine hundred and ninety-nine thousand (British English) nine hundred ninety-nine thousand (American English)
1,000,000	one million

Intermediate numbers are read differently depending on use. In spoken English the term "oh" is also used for the digit zero ("0"). Compare the following:

	How many sheep do you have?	Which bus goes to the railway station?	Alternative (particularly in the US)
101	a hundred and one	one-oh-one	
147	a hundred and forty-seven	one-four-seven	
220	two hundred and twenty	two-two-oh	two-twenty

405	four hundred and five	four-oh-five	
595	five hundred and ninety-five	five-nine-five	five-ninety-five

Other useful numerical expressions

+1.23%	Plus one point two three percent
-27.6%	Minus twenty-seven point six percent
< €3.9M	Less than three point nine million euros
> $55,000	More / greater than fifty-five thousand dollars
¼	One-quarter (US: one-fourth)
	Three-eighths
2009 (year)	Two thousand (and) nine (also twenty oh nine)
2020	Two thousand (and) twenty

Currencies

In spoken English we use the plural of all currencies:

- Twenty-five dollars
- Ten thousand pounds
- Five hundred and forty-one euros
- Forty thousand roubles
- Seven thousand yen (*singular and plural*)

But note the following:

- A twenty-pound concert ticket
- A five-thousand dollar deposit
- A three-point-five million euro property

English phonetic spelling

When speaking on the telephone, it is often necessary to spell words using English phonetic spelling, for example your name and address.

There are several different versions originating from different organisations and English-speaking countries. However, in each case the names for the letters are based on a combination of things like dances (foxtrot, tango), Shakespeare (Romeo & Juliet), men's first names (Charlie, Mike, Oscar, Victor) and cities (Lima, Quebec).

Example

"My name is Mertl: That's Mike, Echo, Romeo, Tango, Lima."

Your own phonetic spelling

If you can't remember all of the names in the table, you can use some of your own. But remember: all names must be well-known and easily understood by English speakers! Practice spelling your name, address and company name a few times and you'll be amazed how easy it is to remember all the names.

	English phonetic spelling	Letter name (IPA) – for pronunciation only
A	Alpha	A
B	Bravo	bee
C	Charlie	cee
D	Delta	dee
E	Echo	E
F	Foxtrot	ef
G	Golf	gee
H	Hotel	aitch or haitch
I	India	I
J	Juliet	jay
K	Kilo	kay
L	Lima	el
M	Mike	em
N	November	en
O	Oscar	O
P	Papa	pee
Q	Quebec	cue
R	Romeo	ar
S	Sierra	ess
T	Tango	tee
U	Uniform	U
V	Victor	vee
W	Whisky	double-u
X	X-ray	ex
Y	Yankee	wy (sometimes written wye)
Z	Zulu	zed; zee in US English

English around the world

This TaschenGuide uses British English and spelling. American (US) English is also very common in international business. Other English-speaking countries (particularly Australia, Canada and New Zealand) also use their own particular spellings and expressions. For the non-native speaker this can be an additional complication. Here are a few tips:

- Check what your company's policy is! Many global organisations prefer American English. Many organisations with strong connections with the UK or its former colonies prefer British English. Most word processing software also offers other versions (Australian, Canadian, Indian etc.).
- Make sure that the spellchecker on your computer is set to the appropriate type of English you decide to use. You may receive documents where another type of English has been preset or another language has been set by default.
- British English allows both the use of "s" and "z" in some words, where as in the US, only "z" is used (e.g. rationalise or rationalize).
- Be consistent. Try not to mix spellings, vocabulary or idioms.
- In many English-speaking countries, neutral titles are replacing most job titles which have historically used "man". Here are a few important examples:
  chair or chairperson (*rather than chairman*), supervisior (*rather than foreman*), police officer (*rather than policeman*), fire-fighter (*rather than fireman*), spokesperson (*rather than spokesman*), manager (*for both men and women*).

Index

Bibliografische Information der Deutschen Nationalbibliothek
Die Deutsche Nationalbibliothek verzeichnet diese Publikation in der Deutschen Nationalbibliografie; detaillierte bibliografische Daten sind im Internet über http://www.d-nb.de abrufbar.

ISBN 978-3-648-01760-9
Bestell-Nr. 00962-0002

2. Auflage 2012

Redaktionsanschrift: Fraunhoferstraße 5, 82152 Planegg
Fon (0 89) 8 95 17-0, Fax (0 89) 8 95 17-2 50
E-Mail: online@haufe.de
Internet: www.haufe.de
Redaktion: Jürgen Fischer
Redaktionsassistenz: Christine Rüber

Konzeption und Realisation: Sylvia Rein, 81371 München
Lektorat: Otto von Dehn, 46348 Raesfeld; Sylvia Rein, 81371 München
Umschlaggestaltung: Kienle gestaltet, 70178 Stuttgart
Umschlagentwurf: Agentur Buttgereit & Heidenreich, 45721 Haltern am See

Druck: freiburger graphische betriebe, 79108 Freiburg

Der Autor

Stuart Dean

ist selbständiger Englisch-Trainer, Coach und Übersetzer bei verschiedenen renommierten Unternehmen. Nach seinem Studium der Betriebswirtschaft in Großbritannien war er mehrere Jahre im Bereich Marketing auf internationaler Ebene tätig. Er verfügt über umfassende kaufmännische und interkulturelle Erfahrung.

Internet: www.stuartdean.de

Weitere Literatur

„E-Mails in English", von Sander M. Schroevers, 128 Seiten, € 6,90, ISBN 978-3-648-01249-9, Bestell-Nr. 00975

„Die besten Bewerbungsmuster Englisch", von Lisa Förster, 156 Seiten, mit CD-ROM, € 19,80
ISBN 978-3-448-08781-9, Bestell-Nr. 04078

„Controlling-Fachbegriffe Deutsch-Englisch, Englisch-Deutsch", von Anette Bosewitz, mit CD-ROM, € 29,80
ISBN 978-3-448-06030-0, Bestell-Nr. 01418

Haufe TaschenGuides

Kompakte Informationen zum kleinen Preis

Der Betrieb in Zahlen

- ABC des Finanz- und Rechnungswesens
- Balanced Scorecard
- Betriebswirtschaftliche Formeln
- Bilanzen
- BilMoG
- Buchführung
- Businessplan
- BWL Grundwissen
- BWL kompakt
- Controllinginstrumente
- Deckungsbeitragsrechnung
- Einnahmen-Überschussrechnung
- Englische Wirtschaftsbegriffe
- Finanz- und Liquiditätsplanung
- Finanzkennzahlen und Unternehmensbewertung
- Formelsammlung Betriebswirtschaft
- Formelsammlung Wirtschaftsmathematik
- IFRS
- Kaufmännisches Rechnen
- Kennzahlen
- Kontieren und buchen
- Kostenrechnung
- So funktioniert die Wirtschaft
- Statistik
- VWL Grundwissen

Mitarbeiter führen

- Besprechungen
- Delegieren
- Checkbuch für Führungskräfte
- Führungstechniken
- Die häufigsten Managementfehler
- Management
- Mitarbeitergespräche
- Moderation
- Motivation
- Neu als Chef
- Projektmanagement
- Qualitätsmanagement
- Spiele für Workshops und Seminare
- Teams führen
- Workshops
- Zielvereinbarungen und Jahresgespräche

Karriere

- Assessment Center
- Existenzgründung
- Gründungszuschuss
- Jobsuche und Bewerbung
- Vorstellungsgespräche

Geld und Specials

- Sichere Altersvorsorge
- Börse
- Energie sparen im Haushalt
- Geldanlage von A–Z
- Immobilien erwerben
- Immobilienfinanzierung
- Meine Ansprüche als Rentner
- Eher in Rente
- Web 2.0
- Zitate für Beruf und Karriere
- Zitate für besondere Anlässe

Persönliche Fähigkeiten

- Ihre Ausstrahlung
- Burnout
- Business-Knigge
- Mit Druck richtig umgehen
- Emotionale Intelligenz
- Entscheidungen treffen